$34.95

COLLEGE DEANS
Leading From Within

Mimi Wolverton and
Walter H. Gmelch

AMERICAN COUNCIL ON EDUCATION
ORYX PRESS
Series on Higher Education
2002

The rare Arabian Oryx is believed to have inspired the myth of the unicorn. This desert antelope became virtually extinct in the early 1960s. At that time, several groups of international conservationists arranged to have nine animals sent to the Phoenix Zoo to be the nucleus of a captive breeding herd. Today, the Oryx population is over 1,000, and over 500 have been returned to the Middle East.

Library of Congress Cataloging-in-Publication Data

Wolverton, Mimi.
    College deans : leading from within / Mimi Wolverton and Walter H. Gmelch.
        p. cm.—(American Council on Education/Oryx Press series on higher education)
    Includes bibliographical references and index.
    ISBN 1–57356–394–3 (alk. paper)
    1. Deans (Education)—United States.   2. Universities and colleges—United States—Administration.   I. Gmelch, Walter.   II. Title.   III. Series.
LB2341.W5716   2002
378.1'11—dc21   2001058787

British Library Cataloguing in Publication Data is available.

Library of Congress Catalog Card Number: 2001058787
ISBN: 1–57356–394–3

First published in 2002

Oryx Press, 88 Post Road West, Westport, CT 06881
An imprint of Greenwood Publishing Group, Inc.
www.oryxpress.com

Printed in the United States of America

The paper used in this book complies with the Permanent Paper Standard issued by the National Information Standards Organization (Z39.48–1984).

10 9 8 7 6 5 4 3 2 1

CONTENTS

ACKNOWLEDGMENTS

First, we wish to thank the deans who participated in this study. Without them, there would be no book, and without their willingness to sacrifice their scholarship and personal lives, there would be no college leadership. Second, a study of this magnitude requires a collaborative effort, and we want to acknowledge the contributions made by the research team. Mark Hermanson and Marvin L. Wolverton helped to formulate the original design of the study and to construct the survey instrument. Mark prepared the database and Marv worked on the initial analysis of the data. Joni Montez also worked as a researcher on the project in its latter stages. Finally, we especially appreciate the attention, guidance, encouragement, and help that we received from our reviewers and editors at Oryx Press and Greenwood Publishing–Susan Slesinger, John Murray, Lynn Taylor, and Betty Pessagno.

Teamwork doesn't just happen, and successfully co-directing a major project requires total trust, selflessness, and openness. Before acknowledging others who contributed both personally and professionally to the completion of this book, both authors wish to extend appreciation to each other. Mimi thanks Walt for involving her in the project and for his mentorship and friendship. Walt expresses his sincere gratitude for Mimi's patience while his deanship distracted him from his full attention to the project, for her perseverance in keeping him on course, and friendship and support through the times of transition. Although it was easy to stay the course as they worked together daily at the same university, along the path to completion of this book both authors found themselves at new universities with new challenges. What they have built over the process of conducting the research and writing this book is a lifelong friendship and complementary respect for each other's strengths and perspectives.

Mimi also thanks her father, John Hiatt, who taught her what it means to be a leader; her husband, Marv, for his encouragement and support and for keeping her on the straight and narrow; and Dick Richardson, who always said she could do whatever she set her mind to doing. Over the years, a host of others have served as mentors, models, and friends. Mimi thanks Gary Krahenbuhl, Larry Penley, Nick Appleton, Laura Rendón, Mary Gardiner, Joni Montez, Jo Washburn, Sue Durrant, Paula Gmelch, Susan Poch, Bernard Young, Romero Jalomo, Mario Martinez, Gordon Gates, Lee Jones, Ann Wolverton, and Steve Wolverton for their wise counsel, friendship, inspiration, and faith in her ability.

Walt realizes that although it is customary to acknowledge those who have made a direct contribution, others in his life have immensely impacted his personal and professional development. Most important, he expresses his love and appreciation to his wife, Paula, who supported and encouraged him through the transition from one deanship to another, and to his sons, Ben and Tom, who remain personally close and part of his life even though they live on the West and East Coasts, far from Iowa. Personally, the friendship that Walt and Paula Gmelch have shared with Marv and Mimi Wolverton has added joy and fun to this project and those to come. Finally, Walt would like to thank his best friend, Val Miskin, and his mentors, role models, and closest friends for what they have contributed to the profession and the education of educators: Dale Andersen, Allan Brown, Ken Erickson, Keith Gordon, George and Sharon Gmelch, Tuli Glasman, Irene Hecht, Mary Lou Higgerson, James Sarros, Peter Seldin, Bill Walsh, and the dozens of his dedicated colleagues—and academic leaders at Washington State University, Iowa State University, and other universities who serve the education profession with integrity and vision.

PREFACE

In the academic anatomy of institutions of higher learning, deans provide the delicate but crucial backbone of university decision making. They, more than any other academic administrators, link central administration with academic departments. On the one hand, they serve as extensions of the presidency. On the other hand, many regard them as extensions of the faculty.

In essence, deans are caught between the expectations of their colleges' departments and those of central administration (Baldridge, 1971; Fagin, 1997). Each group, because its success depends on the dean's performance, develops beliefs about what deans should and should not do (Kahn, Wolfe, Quinn, & Snoek, 1964; Stein & Trachtenberg, 1993). These expectations shape perceptions and understandings of the roles in which deans engage. In other words, the role of dean, and how it gets enacted, is influenced by social norms and external exigencies, by the perceptions of those who interact with deans, and by personal abilities (Biddle & Thomas, 1966).

Deans walk a tenuous administrative tightrope. They head professional bureaucracies (colleges) within professional bureaucracies (universities) (Ryan, 1980). As deans within universities, they hold legitimate authority, but within their colleges such direct power can rarely be exercised. Here deans function as disciplinary experts, who happen to be carrying out administrative tasks, among other disciplinary experts. From the university's perspective, the more direct and decisive deans act, the more effective they are. From the college's perspective, such direct use of power is liable to bring a dean down.

The premise that drives this book lies in the authors' firm belief that deans make a difference in their colleges and that their leadership, or lack thereof, will increasingly influence the effectiveness and well-being of the colleges they lead and the universities in which they work. This book examines who the college deans are, how they define their jobs, their perceptions of leadership, the stressors they face, the challenges they encounter, and the trade-offs deans and their universities must make if deans are to be successful leaders.

THE STUDY

College Deans is based on a study conducted by the Center for Academic Leadership at Washington State University.[1] The Center surveyed more than 1,300 academic deans at 360 universities in the United States; 60 percent responded (Gmelch, Wolverton, Wolverton & Hermanson, 1996).[2] Sample institutions came from one of the following three groupings of Carnegie classifications: research, comprehensive, and baccalaureate. Sixty public and sixty private institutions were randomly selected from each Carnegie category. Deans at community colleges were not included in this study because, unlike deans at universities who are subordinate to chief academic officers and whose locus of control is somewhat discipline-specific, deans of instruction at community colleges fulfill functional roles across disciplines. This particular role serves as a better counterpart to that of the university provost than it does to the college dean. At each of the sample institutions, the deans of the colleges of education, business, liberal arts, and allied health professions (primarily nursing) were asked to complete the survey. In some instances, we included colleges where liberal arts and sciences were combined, but we excluded colleges that were devoted solely to the sciences. We also excluded any college that would not be found at institutions in each of the three Carnegie categories (e.g., we omitted colleges of medicine, law, engineering, and agriculture). We included colleges of nursing and public health in a purposeful attempt to increase the number of female respondents. The resulting database includes deans' personal and institutional demographic specifics, their perceptions of role conflict and ambiguity, views of the responsibilities associated with the position, perceptions of job-related stress and the factors associated with it, and understanding of leadership.

THE DEANS

The responses received generated a relatively well-balanced sample, especially in terms of gender and institution type. Of the responding deans, 41 percent were women. Roughly 12 percent of the respondents held minority status, with African-Americans constituting more than half of this segment of the sample. Of the survey respondents, 58 percent worked in public institutions, 42 percent in private universities. One-third were deans in research universities (44 percent of this subgroup were female); 46 percent were at comprehensive universities (38 percent female); the remaining 21 percent were located at baccalaureate institutions (42 percent female). The distribution of deans with minority status across institution types mirrored that of the overall sample.

More than 40 percent worked at universities located in urban areas; about 30 percent were in rural institutions; the remainder classified their universities as suburban. Of the total responses, 29 percent of the deans were housed in colleges or schools of education, 29 percent in liberal arts, 23 percent in nursing or public health, and 18 percent in business. College size varied. On average, 85 full-time faculty and 46 adjunct faculty served 1,700 undergraduate and 400 graduate-level students. About 60 percent of the faculty in these colleges were tenured. Administratively, colleges operated with seven department chairpersons and one or more associate deans. Women tended to head slightly smaller colleges than did their male counterparts.

Deans, on average, were fifty-four years old and had served in their current positions for 5.6 years. Less than 10 percent were under the age of forty years; less than 5 percent were sixty-five years of age or older. Sixteen percent of the respondents had served in their positions for one year or less. Only 12.8 percent had been deans for more than ten years. Women in the position were slightly younger and, with the exception of nursing deans, had served in their positions for less time. Eighty-two percent of them were married; the majority (52 percent) still had children living at home. About two-thirds of responding deans were dissatisfied with their current personal research productivity. Overwhelmingly, however, most (more than 90 percent) believed that their universities were good places to work. Fifty-five percent had mentors. Fifty-seven percent of all the respondents were inside appointments. The majority of responding deans (59 percent) viewed themselves as being both administrators and faculty. A smaller percentage (34 percent) categorized themselves as administrators; relatively few (7 percent) classified themselves solely as faculty. Most believed that they had been hired to bring about change (34 percent) or to help the college deal with growth (20 percent). Eleven percent thought that they had been chosen to deal with crisis; another 28 percent understood their role as sustaining current college programs. Only 7 percent believed that they had been hired because they had been willing to serve as interim dean. Personally, they also believed that they were selected because of their (a) personal rep-utation, (b) administrative experience, (c) scholarship, (d) political acuity, and (e) fund-raising ability (in rank order). Very few felt that gender or eth-nicity played a major role in their selection. Overwhelmingly, they became deans because they wanted to contribute to and improve their colleges.

THE ORGANIZATION OF THE BOOK

College Deans is organized around nine general themes. Chapter 1 intro-duces readers to a typical dean's work day. Chapter 2 explores the back-ground of deans and their movement into the position. In chapter 3, the authors describe the deans' understanding of academic leadership. Chap-ters 4 and 5 examine the roles in which deans engage and the stressors that impact their ability to be effective leaders. The authors then turn to the deans' perceptions of organizational commitment and any intention to leave that they might harbor, and the relationship between these con-structs and the environmental variables deemed important by deans (chapter 6). Three personal resources—confidence, competence, and credibility—that appear to be necessary precursors to effective leadership are examined in chapter 7. Chapter 8 addresses three primary balance is-sues of deans. Finally, chapter 9 presents a model for dean leadership devel-opment and identifies personal, institutional, and professional strategies that promote such development.

NOTES

1. The Center is sponsored and partially funded by the University Council on Educational Administration (UCEA). After this study, the Center was first housed jointly at Washington State University and Iowa State University. It is now at the University of Nevada, Las Vegas, and Iowa State University.

2. Research instruments used in the survey include the Dean's Stress Inven-tory—(Gmelch et al., 1996), Role Conflict and Role Ambiguity Questionnaire (Rizzo, House, & Lirtzman, 1970), Dean's Task Inventory (Gmelch et al., 1996), Satisfaction with Dean's Role (Gmelch et al., 1996), Dean's Leadership Inven-tory (Rosenbach & Sashkin, 1995) and demographic and contextual variables (Gmelch et al., 1996).

PART 1

Deans—Their Campuses and Colleges

CHAPTER

The Deanship

7:00 A.M., Dean Morgan checks his e-mail messages, scanning quickly in search of any potential time bombs waiting to explode during the ensuing day. He finds none.

7:30, he hurriedly thumbs through a file marked "budgetary concerns," one holding the agenda for a 9:00 A.M. deans' council meeting, and another labeled "tribal initiatives," which instead contains wish lists from three college departments.

7:45, he checks his meeting maker only to discover that he has fifteen minutes to get across campus to the College of Agriculture for a meeting he swears wasn't on his calendar yesterday afternoon when he last checked.

8:00 to 9:00, he attends a meeting with the dean of agriculture and learns that the agriculture college is seeking a massive federal grant and would like Dean Morgan's college to collaborate on it.

9:00 to 11:00, attends a deans' council meeting (agenda and notes still sitting on his office desk), at which the deans are directed to cut their college budgets by 5 percent, retroactive six months.

11:00 to 11:15, he hurries back to the college, thinking briefly of his earlier conversation with the agriculture dean and wondering what initiatives and which tribes he's supposed to know about.

11:15 to 11:45, he visits with several faculty who catch him in the hall as he is attempting to enter his office.

11:45 to noon, he quickly reads through his messages and leaves them on his to-do pile.

noon to 1:30 P.M., takes a potential donor to lunch.

1:45 to 2:30, he gets an update on morning college activities. He finds out that while he was out of the office, one student filed a sexual harassment complaint against a college faculty member, claiming that she made unwanted advances with sexual overtones toward the student; another has written an editorial in a highly visible newspaper saying that what goes on in the classroom is totally irrelevant to what takes place in the work world; and, somehow, no classroom was scheduled for a freshman course and sixty students and their instructor had to meet in the hall.

2:30 to 3:30, he signs fifteen letters and memos, trusting his administrative assistant's word that they are routine, that the content is correct, and that he has already agreed to all the stipulations listed in them. He reads and revises four more letters. He notices that the mail contains comments from a potential publisher for a manuscript he submitted several months ago and sees that the reviewers are requesting major revisions. He wonders when he'll get to it—maybe Sunday, three weeks from now. The next two weekends are filled with provost-initiated speaking engagements, meetings with state legislators, and annual fund-raising events.

3:30 to 4:00, he meets with a faculty delegation clamoring for computer upgrades, expensive software, and digital imaging equipment.

4:00 to 4:30, he returns seven phone calls, all marked urgent.

4:30 to 5:30, he meets with the finance officer about the 5 percent budget reduction. He sets a meeting with department chairpersons and directors to discuss the budget.

5:30 to 5:45, he scans a *Chronicle* article that shows his college ranked in the top 20 nationally.

5:45 to 6:30, he deals with a memo from the president asking him to respond to a state legislator's claim that an inordinate amount of money is being wasted because tenured faculty are "retiring on the job" and to write a rejoinder to the legislator's proposal to tie funding to post-tenure reviews.

6:30 to 7:30, he looks through the tenure and promotion file of a faculty member who is courting the notion of filing a racial discrimination charge against the college because she is at risk of not gaining tenure and believes that the college is at fault.

7:30 to 8:30, he responds to forty-four e-mails.

At 8:30 P.M., he says to himself "This has been a pretty typical day—nothing really out of the ordinary happened."

D oes this sound familiar? For deans, it probably does; for others, it may not. If deans are charged with the leadership of their colleges, and the above scenario, in fact, depicts a "typical day," as Dean Morgan calls it, then the deanship has certainly gone awry—not because all the issues addressed in Dean Morgan's day are not important, but because they leave little time for Dean Morgan to actually *lead*. Leading requires time for reflection, professional development, and balance, none of which appear in Dean Morgan's typical day.

DEANS AND THE DEMANDS OF THE DEANSHIP

Deans today face external demands and stressors that were once nonexistent. For example, technological advances give rise to challenges to present-day curricula. Industries specializing in computer-related technology increasingly place demands on universities for curricular reform that focuses on the integration of technology. If universities and their colleges fail to respond, or if their efforts are deemed too little, too late, or too slow, students and potential employers turn to other sources to meet their educational needs. The very technology that drives the curriculum supports a whole new subculture in higher education—the virtual university—and continually expands the influence of another—the for-profit, postsecondary enterprise. Indeed, distance learning and Internet education compete with traditional universities for students who were once their exclusive purview.

Funding agencies too are swayed by industry. They fall in line when potential employers question the efficacy of curricula and accuse universities of fiscal waste and curricular irrelevancy (Jacobson, 1994). Public distrust strains the once ironclad American assumption that a college education is a social good (Mortenson, 1994a), and state legislatures and private funding sources continually look for alternative places to spend their money (Association of Governing Boards of Universities and Colleges, 1996; California Higher Education Policy Center, 1994; Mortenson, 1994b; Stanton, 1990).

To complicate matters further, colleges and universities no longer serve a homogeneous constituency. Some students are older. Quite often, these newer entrants attend parttime, work fulltime, and have family responsibilities. They may be first-generation college-goers, but most certainly have come to college expecting to be equipped for a new career and a better lifestyle. They connect learning to work and want universities to do the same (Scott & Awbrey, 1993). Traditional-age students have also changed. These students grew up on a healthy dose of electronically induced stimuli,

MTV, Nintendo, and complex video games. They learn differently and expect faculty to address their learning needs creatively (Astin, 1993; Baker & Gloster, 1994; Carnegie Foundation, 1990; Latta, 1996). In addition, today, women outnumber men on college campuses across the country, and we see a discernible shift in America's racial makeup, which will ultimately dictate who attends college. In the 1960s, people of color constituted less than 15 percent of the country's total population. By 1990, the size of this segment increased to 20 percent and by the turn of the century neared 30 percent (Astin, 1993; Kerr, Gade, & Kawaoka, 1994a; Levine & Cureton, 1998). In each instance, culturally ingrained assumptions, practices, and general approaches to learning and interacting with others bring tensions to the college, which can either benefit or hamstring efforts to educate America's future workforce.

Change surrounds us. We hear about the need to address change, the imperative that universities and colleges change, why change in the academy will be difficult, and the key role that leaders play in making it happen (Guskin, 1994a, 1994b; Kerr et al., 1994b; Layzell, Lovell, & Gill, 1996). But what is leadership? And how are college deans involved?

DEANS AS LEADERS

College deans engage in four very broadly defined activities. The first three—planning, organizing, and controlling—fall squarely in the management camp and help to operationally define how colleges function on a daily basis. In planning, deans make sense of the means and ends of college business. They set goals and determine (sometimes collaboratively with college members) how the college will go about achieving them. Organizing refers to prioritizing tasks and determining which ones will be grouped together and who will have the responsibility and authority to carry them out. Controlling ensures that actual outcomes are consistent with planned ones, and if not, what went wrong. Control mechanisms at a dean's disposal include hiring, evaluation, and resource allocation. For instance, suppose a college wants to pursue two large projects: one involves infusing some new technology into the curriculum, the other consists of developing a summer institute for budding scholars in the field. Both enterprises carry merit, but the college has enough personnel to pursue only one of them at this time. Left to their own devices, some faculty and staff might choose to work on the technology project and others on the institute. In doing so, the college will very likely be unable to complete either endeavor in a timely manner, nor will the end results reflect the greatest potential the college has to offer. A dean might set each as a goal but then prioritize them based on the immediacy of the need. The task can be broken into smaller segments, and faculty and staff may be given the responsibility and the resources to accomplish their respective pieces. For example, if technology infusion received attention first, mechanisms would have to be put in place to determine whether the project reached its fruition and was successful (or at least was well underway) before the college moved on to planning the summer institute. Deans engage in these managerial endeavors to maintain consistency in the college across time. Such responsibilities consume most deans' time.

Effective deans in today's dynamic environment find they must go a step beyond, however. In the example above, a dean and his or her college must determine how each endeavor relates to the college's future and, given the future, whether it makes sense to pursue either one. This means that deans must be leaders as well as managers. Leading is the most human-oriented of their four primary roles. Leadership has a transformational quality about it. It involves changing the culture and disrupting the status quo. Deans who lead relate external demands to internal endeavors in a manner that moves their colleges into uncharted waters. They are change leaders.

DEANS AND CHANGE LEADERSHIP

"Producing change is the primary function of leadership" (Carr, Hard, & Trahant, 1996, p.116; see also Kotter, 1990a, 1990b; Wolverton, 1998). Over time, scholars who think and write about change leadership have hit upon certain descriptors—dreamer and seer, communicative, inclusive, action-oriented, integrative, intuitive about people, stable—that they believe help to identify leaders (Carr et al., 1996; Cox, 1994; Guskin, 1996; Kotter, 1990a, 1990b; Sherman, 1996; Peters & Waterman, 1982; O'Toole, 1995).

Dreamers and seers inhabit all corners of a college. In the deanship, dreaming becomes organizationally purposeful. It has two dimensions, telescopic and panoramic: telescopic, in that change telegraphs the college into the future; panoramic, because the kind of change that today's deans face cannot be piecemeal but must be comprehensive, broad, and systemwide. Together these dimensions frame a vision, or general notion, of where a college needs to head (Guskin, 1994a, 1994b, 1996; O'Toole, 1995). Deans involved in change dream, but they also remain pragmatic enough to question their assumptions and to continually review their take on reality and the values that undergird it (O'Toole, 1995).

There are two sides to leadership *communication*: listening and relaying. Listening involves paying attention to constituencies, gleaning not only ideas but concerns. Peters and Waterman note that one of leadership's fundamental roles is that of creating a "learning environment" where leaders and those they serve hear each other (1982, p. 283). Within such an environment, deans build trust and demonstrate respect for those with whom they work. Candor and honesty play important roles in determining how successful a dean is in establishing a listening environment. Relaying refers to communication in the more traditional sense: transmitting in an understandable way the why, what, and how of change. Good communication, through ongoing training efforts, regular staff updates, newsletters and the like, maintains momentum (Cox, 1994; O'Toole, 1995).

To be *inclusive* implies a willingness to step aside and allow others to bring more of themselves into their work and problem solving. It also suggests that leaders let subordinates take credit for successes (Sherman, 1995). Change leaders think not so much about what others can or should do, but about what they themselves should stop doing so that others have the opportunity to contribute (O'Toole, 1995). Structurally, the notion of inclusiveness infers a "cascading" of leadership throughout an organization with links between levels that are interwoven into the fabric of institutional operations (Carr et al., 1996).

The attribute that most clearly separates purposeful dreamers—leaders of change—from the rest of the dreamers is their inclination toward *action*. Deans who are change leaders realize that organizations, and they themselves, must learn as they go. They have a sense of direction. They do not require that every minute detail of the journey be known and a plan for every contingency be in place before they begin. These deans keep change moving (Carr et al., 1996; Guskin, 1996; O'Toole, 1995; Peters & Waterman, 1982).

Change leaders think in *integrative* terms—operationally and structurally. Operationally, they understand the benefits that accrue to an organization from involving people from multiple constituencies (especially those who will later be charged with implementation) in the planning phases of the change process. With widespread participation, change goals are more likely to be held in common and resistance lessened. Structurally, deans who are change leaders believe that substantive change occurs only when its processes become fully integrated into the way the college does business—never in isolation, never as an add-on program (Carr et al., 1996; O'Toole, 1995).

Change causes stress. *Intuitive* deans size up people—their strengths, their shortcomings, their willingness to exploit the former, and their ability to overcome the latter. They sense the anxiety that delegating decision-making responsibilities brings, both for those not used to taking on responsibility and for those who are not accustomed to giving it away. In effect, deans who are good change leaders are good people-readers (Carr et al., 1996; Kotter, 1990a; O'Toole, 1995).

In a world of change, how do organizations maintain *stability?* In large part, they do it through leadership. Today, in periods of change, a college that retains its leadership core from change inception to institutionalization stands less chance of becoming sidelined or derailed than do colleges that experience frequent leadership turnover (Carr et al., 1996; Cox, 1994; Guskin, 1996; O'Toole, 1995). In environments that move slowly in anticipated patterns and that forgive organizational inertia, overreliance on custom, and a tendency to preserve the status quo, change becomes predictable and relatively easy. If one dean replaces another in midstream, little disruption occurs, and things move along very much as they have in the past. In contrast, change in a dynamic environment fraught with uncertainty becomes more radical and its consequences patently more severe. Because systemic change efforts can take ten to fifteen years and require continuity of thought and direction, change initiatives in this environment can easily disappear. For organizations like colleges, where deans often remain at the same institution no more than six years (and new leadership frequently brings with it a fresh agenda and a different leadership team), this usually means trouble (Guskin, 1996).

DEAN MORGAN AS LEADER

We can readily see the basic elements of change in Dean Morgan's day. Dealing with budgetary and fund-raising issues, pursuing collaborative initiatives across colleges, ensuring curricular relevance, and making diversity work all suggest not just current managerial problems or crises—fires to be put out—but opportunities to be fueled that could and probably will change the future of the college. To see beyond the fire to the future, Dean Morgan needs time to think and reflect.

Noticeably absent from Dean Morgan's day is any mention of dreaming or seeing the big picture. He appears mired in and conditioned by the tasks of keeping the college running. He reacts to the environment, but we get little sense that he has the time or inclination to evaluate the college's current direction to determine whether it needs to be changed. To do so requires that he spend time thinking about the college's possibilities—not just one or five years from now, but ten years down the road. Over time, he must be able to interact with people in and outside the college to gain a grasp of what its true potential might be.

In higher education, we make a very large assumption that the deans hired by colleges possess the skills and aptitudes they need to be successful. However, skills are learned and aptitudes honed through professional development activities for which many deans have little time. In Dean Morgan's case, time for professional development appears to be in short supply. If Dean Morgan's day is typical, then there simply is no room for professional development. He must, in essence, fend for himself.

In examining his typical day we also have to ask ourselves, does he have a personal life—friends, family, activities outside work? Mental and physical health depend on being able to maintain balance. Some people can sustain imbalance for fairly long periods of time, but the end result for many is often stress, frustration, burnout, and ultimately dropout. Dean Morgan's day at the office begins before 8:00 A.M. and ends after 8:00 P.M. His weekends appear to be filled with work-related over-run—fund raising, politicking, and proselytizing. Does he ever catch himself saying, "I couldn't do this job if I had a life"? In retrospect, will he exclaim, "Gee, I wish I'd spent more time at the office"?

Colleges and universities have always faced change and dealt with it. Over time, American universities have moved from preparing very few for elite leadership roles to educating the masses. Colleges and universities have, over the past thirty years, implemented and institutionalized more systematic ways of planning and budgeting. They are no longer perceived as ivory towerish as they once were. Curricula and programs do fall under periodic review, but colleges have had the luxury, or the good fortune, to be able to change at their own pace—slowly, incrementally, with little interference from the outside.

In an environment where change now appears to occur exponentially rather than linearly and predictably, can colleges afford to continue on the same course? We think not. Are today's deans equipped to lead effective organizations tomorrow? Here is a question we cannot answer. We do not know the Dean Morgans of the university world, where they come from, what they do, the pressures they face, or how they perceive the future.

CHAPTER 2

Transition to the Deanship

Where does the road to the deanship begin? In the home? At high school and college? From the teaching ranks in the academy? The metamorphosis that deans experience as they transition from academician to administrator is murky at best, but it is clear from the literature on business executives that the process begins long before an individual reaches the professional ranks of the academy. Researchers suggest that parental expectations in early childhood and youth leadership experiences influence the development of leaders (Boone, Kurtz, & Fleenor, 1988; Forbes & Piercy, 1991). In addition, motivation seems to play a role in how deans transition to the position. Finally, the career path that an academic assumes may have a bearing on dean leadership. Once deans make the decision to take the position, they go through a rite of passage. They engage the idea of becoming a dean, pass through three stages (separation, transition, and incorporation), and then reengage as they settle into the deanship (van Gennep, 1960). This chapter examines each of these aspects of moving into the deanship.

EVOLUTION OF THE DEAN:
AN ETHOS AT HOME AND SCHOOLING

One of the most important factors in deans' ascensions to their positions may have little to do with experience as an administrator in or outside the academy; rather, it begins at home. Attitudes about work and school, career goals, and aspirations have a great impact on children's career choices and decisions (Epstein, 1990; Fullan, 1991; Henry, 1996; Lankard, 1995; Moore, 1992; Smith, 1991; Winters, 1993). Research suggests that high-achieving students come from families who hold high educational and occupational expectations for their children (Okagaki & Sternberg, 1993). In general, parents who believe that success in school depends on effort, and not solely on ability, are much more likely to encourage their children to work hard and to participate in activities related to academic achievement and leadership development (Mau, 1997; Wolverton & Poch, 2000). In fact, high school students often cite parental support as why some students excel and others fail (Hearst Newspapers, 1999).

Thinking back to their formative years, almost 70 percent of the deans credited their parents (or guardians) with stressing high standards of excellence. In fact, women and minorities were significantly more likely to classify their parents in this manner than were white males, whose parents were interested in their achievement but satisfied with average performance. Few (3 percent) suggested that parents were not interested in or hindered their progress at school.

In addition to parental expectations, participation in social organizations and student government activities helps young people to develop their leadership abilities (Kleon & Rinehart, 1998). Leadership practice and experience in one's early years prepares people for future roles as leaders in the workplace. Student government prepares politicians; literary organizations help to fine-tune communication skills; clubs, fraternities, and sororities offer arenas in which interpersonal skills can be enhanced; athletics builds team players; service organizations create a sense of social responsibility or servant leadership (Greenleaf, 1977)—all attributes and skills used by deans.

During their high school and college years, deans in the study assumed leadership roles in numerous extracurricular activities. Of these activities, they tended to accept leadership roles more in community-oriented activities—such as student government (46 percent), service organizations (50 percent), and club activities (50 percent)—than in pursuits that require individual prowess or wherewithal, such as literary or newspaper efforts, which require writing and editing skills (30 percent); athletics, which demand coordination and ability (30 percent); or fraternities and sororities, where membership may depend on popularity or access to money (20 percent). Male deans had been more active in athletics than had female deans; this may have been because many women in this study attended high school and college between 1950 and 1970, when athletics for girls was virtually nonexistent. Instead, women tended to be more active in newspapers, service organizations, and clubs—leadership venues more equitably open to them. On the whole, minority deans assumed significantly more leadership roles than their white counterparts. Although no one activity proved common to all our deans, 73 percent of the deans took a leadership role in at least one service, social, or literary organization. Table 2.1 illustrates these trends.

Collectively, deans took on leadership roles early in life, with a tendency to engage more in community or service leadership activities. This, in combination with high parental expectations, appears to have provided them with the bedrock upon which future leadership endeavors are developed (Wolverton & Poch, 2000).

PERSONAL MOTIVATION: TO SERVE OR NOT TO SERVE

Entry into the deanship starts from somewhere. Professors, like schoolteachers, have two options as they enter the academy. They can establish a career within their discipline, or they may decide to "try their hand" at academic administration. Since most academicians do not enter the academy with administration in mind, what motivates them to become administrators in the first place? Most are first called into leadership to serve as department chairpersons. Some chairpersons serve for extrinsic reasons: their deans or colleagues convinced them to take the job, or they feel forced to take it because no one else is willing to take on the responsibility or can do the job properly. In contrast, other chairpersons seek the position for intrinsic reasons: they see it as an opportunity to help either the department or themselves professionally.

Table 2.1
Dean Leadership Roles in High School or College

	Overall % Participated	Men	Women	Minority
Service Organizations	.50	.44	.60	.74
Club Activities	.50	.45	.59	.61
Student Government	.46	.47	.44	.54
Literary/News	.30	.23	.39	.37
Fraternity/Sorority	.20	.19	.20	.31
Athletics	.30	.38	.19	.26

For department chairpersons, the initial motivation to serve, whether intrinsic or extrinsic, significantly impacts their long-term commitment to service as academic leaders. Of those serving for extrinsic reasons, only one-fourth are willing to serve another term, in contrast to three-fourths of those who were intrinsically motivated (Gmelch & Miskin, 1993). In addition, some simply enjoy research more, like teaching better, dislike administration (paperwork, negotiating), or see the position as too stressful, time-consuming, political, difficult, and disassociated from their disciplines (McCarty & Reyes, 1987). Table 2.2 shows a breakdown of these reasons.

Most individuals who go on to serve as deans indicate that they desired to contribute to and improve the college (95 percent), sought the deanship for personal growth (83 percent), and wanted to influence the development of faculty (77 percent). Five in ten deans took the position to advance their administrative careers (53 percent). In contrast to these reasons for becoming deans, fewer sought the position for financial gain (25 percent) or the power and authority of the position (20 percent). Women in nursing colleges tended to see these last options as more motivating than did other deans. Table 2.3 details these motivations.

ACADEMIC PATH TO THE DEANSHIP

The conventional pathway to becoming a dean has been characterized as "professional ascension," or rising through the ranks (Morris, 1981). Although Moore and her colleagues (1983) found that the vast majority of deans have been faculty, no particular overarching career trajectory was

Table 2.2
Chairpersons' Reasons for Not Seeking Deanship

Reasons	Time Mentioned	Percent of Total
1. Enjoy research more	18	24.3
2. Like teaching better	17	22.9
3. Dislike administration	16	21.6
4. Position too stressful	5	6.8
5. Decisions too difficult	4	5.4
6. Insufficient leadership opportunities	4	5.4
7. Too time consuming	3	4.1
8. Deal with other people's problems	3	4.1
9. Totally disassociated from discipline	2	2.7
10. Too much politics	2	2.7
Total	74	100.0

Source: McCarty & Reyes, 1987.

Table 2.3
Motivation to Serve as a Dean

	% High	Men	Women	Minority	Business	Education	Liberal Arts	Nursing
Desire to contribute/improve college	.95	.95	.95	.99	.95	.96	.96	.94
Influence faculty development	.83	.74	.83	.76	.68	.79	.81	.80
Personal growth	.77	.81	.86	.86	.79	.83	.80	.89
Advancement of career	.53	.21	.58	.48	.46	.24	.43	.67
Financial gain	.25	.24	.24	.21	.16	.26	.22	.30
Power/authority of position	.20	.18	.28	.17	.19	.15	.16	.32

found to lead to a deanship (See also Twombly, 1986). As a matter of fact, "more deans conform to variations from the 'norms' than to the 'norms' themselves" (Moore, Salimbene, Marlier, & Bragg, 1983, p. 514).

In our study, when deans were asked about administrative experience prior to their current deanship, 30 percent had been deans before, less than 40 percent had been associate deans, more than 60 percent had been department chairpersons, and 18 percent had had administrative experience outside the academy. Men in the study seemed to have had the most experience.

Although increasing numbers of women and minorities are entering the faculty ranks of higher education, it appears that relatively few advance into administrative positions (Turner, Myers, & Creswell, 1997). Few women in the study had prior administrative experience as deans (less than 25 percent) or as associate deans (38 percent). A higher percentage had been department chairwomen (56 percent) before becoming deans. Women came to the deanship with almost as much frequency from other academic positions, such as coordinator or director (35 percent). Few had leadership or administrative experience outside the academy prior to taking the deanship, and most did not move up a chain-of-command type of career ladder (i.e., department chairwoman, associate dean, or dean) to get to the position. Thirty-eight percent of minority-status deans had previous experience as dean before taking their current positions. The majority had been department chairpersons (64 percent). Fewer had been associate deans (24 percent), but 36 percent had held other types of academic positions prior to their current one. Twenty-three percent of these respondents indicated that they had been in senior management positions outside higher education before coming to the deanship. Neither men nor women in this position, in general, nor minority-status deans, in particular, experienced a clear lockstep approach to the deanship. Table 2.4 shows these pathways to deanship.

Table 2.4
Dean Career Paths by Gender and Race

Position	Overall	Male	Female	Minority
Dean, Previous to Current Position	.30	.32	.22	.38
Associate Dean	.40	.35	.38	.24
Department Chair	.60	.66	.56	.64
Other Academic Position	.35	.38	.35	.36
Senior Management Outside H.E.	.18	.17	.20	.23
Previous Dean & Chair	.20	.22	.16	.26
Associate Dean & Chair	.20	.20	.21	.15
Department Chair & Other	.17	.19	.16	.22
Department Chair & Sr. Management	.10	.09	.11	.13

Note: Few deans held both previous and associate deanships, a previous deanship or an associate deanship and another academic leadership position, or a previous deanship and a senior management position prior to taking their current positions.

A higher percentage of deans at research universities than at comprehensive or baccalaureate institutions served as associate deans, and a slightly higher percentage had been both chairpersons and associate deans. Other than that, we found no career paths that were unique to one institution type. When we examined career paths across the four disciplines (liberal arts, business, education, and nursing), however, several interesting patterns emerged (Wolverton & Gonzales, 2000). First, whereas almost 70 percent of the liberal arts deans had been department chairpersons, less than 55 percent of business deans had held the same position. Second, 40 percent of the education deans and 36 percent of those in liberal arts colleges had had some experience in other academic leadership positions. Fewer business and nursing deans had this type of experience. Third, only 8 percent of the liberal arts deans had held senior management positions outside the academy, and only 14 percent of education deans had had such experience. Nursing and business deans, in contrast, were much more likely to have worked outside the academy sometime prior to the deanship (nursing, 27 percent; business, 31 percent). Fourth, more liberal arts, nursing, and education deans had held both associate dean and chairperson positions. From 20 to 25 percent of these deans had served in both capacities. Less than 15 percent of business deans had followed the same trajectory. Finally, business and nursing deans were slightly more likely than others to have been both senior managers outside higher education institutions and department chairpersons within their respective college types. Even with these observations, a strictly hierarchical linear model for the deanship remains unclear. Table 2.5 provides these trends.

The average length of time that deans spent in each of these positions before becoming dean was two years or less, with the exception of those serving about four years as department chairperson. Although it is not evident whether deans matriculate through certain administrative ranks before reaching the deanship, more deans have served as department chairpersons than in any other position, and they hold that position longer than other administrative position. Such findings suggest that the position of department chairperson serves as the most frequent jumping off point for the deanship. Table 2.6 provides these statistics.

Table 2.5
Dean Career Paths (Percentage with Previous Experience)

Position	Overall	Institution Type			Discipline			
		Res.	Comp.	Bac.	Lib. Arts	Business	Education	Nursing
Dean, Previous to Current Position	.30	.31	.32	.20	.30	.32	.33	.28
Associate Dean	.40	.50	.36	.15	.33	.39	.35	.45
Department Chair	.60	.62	.63	.63	.69	.54	.64	.58
Other Academic Position	.35	.32	.33	.37	.36	.29	.40	.28
Senior Management Outside H.E.	.18	.15	.20	.17	.08	.31	.14	.27
Previous Dean & Chair	.20	.19	.21	.15	.21	.18	.23	.15
Associate Dean & Chair	.20	.28	.19	.10	.20	.14	.23	.25
Department Chair & Other	.17	.15	.18	.17	.20	.12	.21	.13
Department Chair & Sr. Management	.10	.06	.11	.11	.05	.13	.08	.14

Table 2.6
Deans' Years of Administrative Experience

| | Average Years | Discipline | | | | Institutional Type | | |
		Liberal Arts	Business	Education	Nursing	Research	Compre-hensive	Bachelors
Years as Dean	5.6	5.3	5.0	5.6	6.6	5.6	5.8	5.4
Years Dean Prior to This Position	1.7	1.7	1.7	2.2	1.5	1.9	2.0	1.1
Years Associate Dean	1.7	1.5	1.9	1.8	2.0	2.4	1.6	.8
Years Department Chair	3.6	4.7	3.2	3.5	3.1	3.2	3.8	3.5
Years Other Academic Admin.	1.5	2.0	2.2	2.9	2.0	2.0	2.2	3.2
Years Manager Outside Acad.	2.3	.5	3.5	1.0	1.8	1.1	1.8	1.7

ENTRY INTO THE DEANSHIP:
THE DEAN'S RITES OF PASSAGE

Academics who opt for a deanship as a career may undergo severe changes (socialization) as they move into administration. New deans find themselves in a transition that demands personal development and creates new learnings. Research on stages of personal development begins with Freud's and Piaget's charting of childhood development and ends with Erikson's stages of adolescence. Until a couple of decades ago, developmental charting stopped around age twenty-one—as if adults escape any further distinguishable stages of development. Three prominent life-cycle scholars—Gould, Levinson, and Vaillant—have reached new conclusions about adulthood. These theories, popularly written about in Sheehy's books *Passages* (1976) and *New Passages* (1995) and professionally reported in Levinson's *The Seasons of a Man's Life* (1978) and Gould's *Transformations* (1978), outline remarkably predictable crises of adulthood. Although there is no shortage of theory from which to base stages of personal development in academia, considerable discrepancy exists among theorists and across disciplinary approaches (Bridges, 1991).

For instance, sociologists label the period from the time of appointment to a position until the time of acceptance in the organization as the *organizational socialization* period. From the many organizational socialization developmental models (Hart, 1993), a similar three-stage model emerges: (a) anticipation, (b) encounter, and (c) adaptation. The *anticipation* stage begins when one has been selected for the new position and has made the decision to leave the current position, breaking off loyalties to the present position and developing new loyalties. Louis (1980) refers to this as leave-taking. The *encounter* stage begins when one actually starts the new position and begins to cope with the routines, surprises, and relationships. Finally, the *adaptation* stage begins when one develops strong trusting relationships in the academy and finds out how things work in the informal organization. This theoretical framework has been used to study new department chairpersons' transition from faculty to administration (Gmelch & Parkay, 1999; Gmelch & Seedorf, 1989; Seedorf, 1990) and new school administrators' socialization process (Ortiz, 1982).

In contrast, traditional tribal societies place tremendous emphasis on transitions in their social culture, just as did ancient civilizations. Van Gennep (1960), a Dutch anthropologist, began interpreting these rites for a modern, Western audience almost eighty-five years ago and coined the term *rites of passage* to describe how rites were used in traditional societies to structure transitions dealing with birth, puberty, death, selection of a chief, and creation of the shaman (see also Bridges, 1980). The first stage consists of a person separating oneself from the old and familiar social context and putting oneself through a symbolic death experience. Next comes a time of isolation in what van Gennep called the "neutral zone," a gap between the old way of being and the new. Finally, when the intended inner changes have taken place, the person is brought back and reenters the social order on a new basis.

Although appointing a new dean is not equivalent to anointing a shaman, Gmelch (2000b), in a self-reflective study, found that dean passage rites revealed the same three-stage process: separation, transition, and incorporation. Figure 2.1 portrays a more complete cycle of the socialization process, which begins with an engagement stage, from which the academic launches into the dean socialization process, then moves through the three stages of socialization—separation, transition and incorporation—and ends with reengagement or settling into the deanship.

Engagement: The Professorial Plateau

As we have noted, most academics do not enter the academy with administration in mind. Department chairpersons tend to be socialized in their disciplines for more than sixteen years before accepting the chairperson position (Carroll, 1991). However, the transition from the professorial plateau into the deanship is different in nature and magnitude than the initial transition from faculty into the administrative roles of department chairperson or associate dean. Most department chairpersons do not strive to permeate the boundaries of administration or seek to be totally socialized into the administrative structure of the university (Gmelch & Miskin, 1993). Many deans do.

Stage 1: Separation

Passage to a deanship begins with letting go of something. It starts at the end of the plateau period—ready to take a plunge, to test the water, to become a full-time administrator. In anticipation of a position in academic leadership, faculty seek formal preparation (professional development conferences, workshops and programs) or informal means of enlisting mentors, such as GASing activities (Getting the Attention of Superiors through committee work, and so on) (Griffiths, 1966). This is vastly different from the anticipatory stage of teachers entering school administration. Two very different types of candidates seek the administrative role in elementary and secondary schools. Most of the candidates consider teaching as a transitional role; that is, they aspired to be a principal when they began teaching; the remainder of candidates enter teaching as teachers and only

Figure 2.1
The New Dean's Rite of Passage

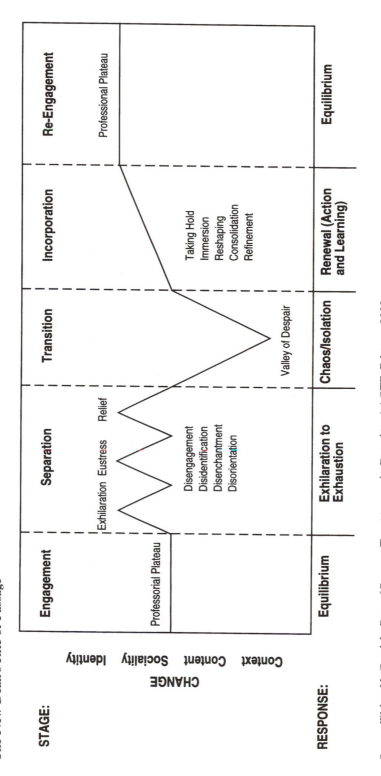

Source: Walter H. Gmelch, *Rites of Passage: Transitions to the Deanship.* AACTE, February 2000.

later move into administration (Blood, 1966). In contrast, professors customarily enter higher education to engage in scholarship and teach in their discipline and are socialized in their discipline for almost two decades (from graduate school through the professorial ranks) before considering a new role in academic administration (Carroll, 1991). Whereas teachers must formally engage in the study of administration to become certified to administer, a discipline-specific Ph.D. is considered sufficient to enter academic administration. As a result, the separation for new deans is filled with mixed emotions: disengagement, disidentification, disenchantment, and disorientation (Bridges, 1980; Gmelch, 2000b).

Disengagement. Traditional peoples universally believe that in times of inner transition people need to be separated from their familiar place in the social order—removed from family and sometimes forcibly taken out into the forest or the desert. The prospective shaman leaves the village on a long trek of self-discovery. Though not shamans, new deans find that the new role creates a disengagement: from close faculty relationships; from scholarship as they knew it as faculty members; from familiar departmental settings to new "distant" dean office settings; and from being a faculty colleague to being a mediator, boundary spanner, and politician. Clarified, channeled, and supported, the change can lead toward development and renewal. However, the dean's development is not focused or formally prescribed by the institution but left to random and informal self-exploration (see chapter 9).

Disidentification. In breaking the old connections to the institution and college, new deans lose familiar ways of self-identification. For some new deans, it means the loss of the faculty role that prescribed their behavior and made them readily identifiable. When department chairpersons are asked who they are, most respond with their faculty identity, whereas more deans reflect their administrative identity. Their identities change from primarily faculty to primarily administrator. Only 7 percent of the deans see themselves primarily as faculty, in contrast to 43 percent of the department chairpersons. Thus, socialization into administration and away from faculty status becomes much more pronounced for deans.

Disenchantment. The discovery that in some sense the role of faculty member is no longer real for them leads to disenchantment. The disenchanted new dean recognizes that the old view was sufficient in its time but is insufficient now. Two-thirds of the deans studied indicated that they had severely reduced their level of scholarship upon becoming a dean, and 61 percent were dissatisfied with that change. Socially, faculty tend to distance themselves from the dean and perceive the new dean as different from a colleague or faculty member. In turn, deans spend more time becoming acclimated in their new social circle of deans, central administrators, and external stakeholders. As a result, new deans lose their identities as scholars and start to feel a sense of isolation from faculty colleagues.

Disorientation. The change affects not only one's sense of space but of time as well. In old passage rituals, the one in transition would often be taken out into unfamiliar territory beyond the bound of his or her experience and left there for a time. The dean moves in new and unfamiliar circles, trading time spent in departmental faculty meetings for provost meetings and unfamiliar engagements with unknown external constituents.

Stage 2: Transition

The transition phase is the time between the old job and the new—a rich time for insight and discovery. It actually begins with the anticipation of a move and continues throughout the phases of incorporation and re-engagement. Rather than a linear depiction as in Figure 2.1 with distinct starting and stopping points for each phase, the phases are more overlap-

Figure 2.2
Three Phases of the New Dean

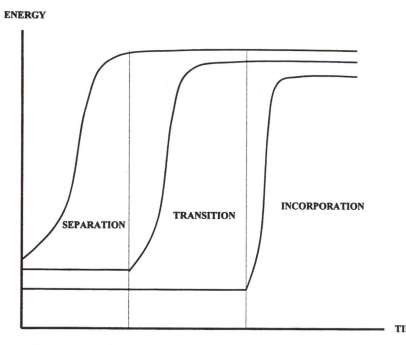

Source: Walter H. Gmelch, Leadership succession: How new deans take charge and learn the job. *Journal of Leadership Studies*, 7(3).

ping where one is dominant at a time but the other phases are still present as suggested in Figure 2.2.

Certain events or ceremonies signal the end of the separation period and the beginning of the transition to the new position. It is a kind of "street-crossing" procedure as deans try not to be in the middle of the street longer than necessary. It is a time when the old way for new deans is gone and the new doesn't feel quite comfortable.

Transition is, in fact, a source of self-renewal, because after deans have struggled and floundered in the separation phase, self-renewal and reflection is needed. The new dean's valley of despair, as depicted in Figure 2.1, represents the time in the middle of the transition period when one finds ways of being alone and away from all the familiar distractions. Just as tribal elders provided tools in the form of rituals, deans in transition must fashion their own tools to help shorten their transitions.

Stage 3: Incorporation

A former dean and renowned anthropologist once reflected, "Being a new dean is like learning to ice skate in full view of your faculty." The assimilation and success can take from a few months to years. Scholars do not agree on its duration. With public school administrators, some visible change and movement into incorporation occurs within three months of a high school principal's succession (Lamoreaux, 1990); with others, change lasts for eighteen months (Weindling & Early, 1987) to two years due to the unique structure of the traditional school year (Cosgrove, 1986). A study of fourteen business management successions concluded that the process of "taking charge" can be long, taking from two to two and a half years—some even longer or not at all (Gabarro, 1985). Similarly, some principals fail to achieve even basic socialization after five years (Parkay & Hall, 1992), and in higher education many department chairpersons enter the anticipatory and encounter stages but do not successfully adapt to their leadership positions (Seedorf, 1990).

The incorporation of a new dean follows a predictable pattern similar to that of corporate executives as they "take charge" of their new positions: (a) taking hold, (b) immersion, (c) reshaping, (d) consolidation, and (e) refinement (Gabarro, 1985; Gmelch, 2000b). While the overall length of time for incorporation is similar, the phases mirrored the structure of the academic year. The following highlights characterize each of the phases of incorporation of the new dean.

Taking Hold. In the business world, this stage lasts three to six months, as it does for new deans. In general, the taking-hold period is characterized by intense learning and uncontrollable activity. This arrival phase requires much learning on the part of a new dean. Cognitive learning focuses on rational interpretations (how things are done around here) and rationales that people construct (why things are done in a particular way). Sometimes this process is called sense making (Louis, 1980). New deans continually ask why things are done a particular way, which challenges institutional assumptions and personal beliefs, thus opening up discussion for innovation and discovery of different methods or strategies. Actions taken during the taking-hold stage tend to be corrective, short-term interventions embarked upon while learning the system.

Immersion. Compared to the taking-hold phase, the second phase appears to be the quiet after the storm. This period creates a chance for more focused learning as the experience base grows and patterns start to emerge. During the immersion stage new deans start to question whether they have the right people in the right places.

Reshaping. External opportunities start to reshape and cause a burst of activity that is equal to the first phase but focused on some clear targets rather than fragmented. The reshaping phase also involves altering some college processes as well as planning some structural shifts in the office. Reshaping ends when the new dean has implemented as many initiatives as circumstances allow. What now stands in the way, as it did in the case of the business executive incorporation, is the availability of personnel for key positions.

Consolidation. The final wave of action occurs in the consolidation phase. New deans' learning and action focus on consolidating and following through on changes contemplated during the reshaping phase. Learning in the consolidation phase centers on two issues. In the first, deans identify implementation problems, and in the second, they discover unanticipated problems and consequences made during the reshaping and implementation phases. Activity during the consolidation phase involves diagnosing problems, then correcting them. Finally, as Gabarro (1985) predicts, the new leaders have to find ways to deal with plans that previously could not, but now can, be implemented.

Refinement. Although new deans are predictably still a few months from the end of this final phase of incorporation, certain aspects of the refinement phase have become apparent. This is a time of little organizational change. It is when "executives have taken charge and their learning and actions tend to focus either on refining operations or on looking for opportunities in the marketplace" (Gabarro, 1985, p. 116). Refinement marks the end of the incorporation stage. It is the point when the dean no longer feels new. In fact, other deans or senior administrators have been hired since the dean's arrival. Faculty and staff no longer speak of or refer to the dean as new. Problems in the college are not attributed to newness but are now "owned" and probably created by the dean. Enough time has passed for the dean to establish credibility, a power base, and a network of colleagues.

Table 2.7 presents a summary of the five phases of incorporation. It is organized according to the primary themes addressed by new deans, the dominant leadership style based on a five-style schematic that they assume during each period (Bolman & Deal, 1991; Hersey & Blanchard, 1988), and their psychological orientation during each of the phases. For instance, when deans take hold, they invest time in people (human resource management). As they become immersed in the college they take charge structurally. In reshaping they become visionary (symbolic). As they consolidate power their actions take on political trappings. Finally, as they refine the position, deans make decisions based on the situation at hand.

Similarly, one new dean in this study felt "settled in" when he perceived that three conditions came together. First, he became *committed* to the institution and college, as indicated by a deep sense of pride in the university's accomplishments and a new loyalty to the institution and his colleagues. Second, he gained a sense of *competence* in what he was doing. He understood the roles and responsibilities of the dean and felt competent in performing his duties. Finally, and only after twenty months in the position, this particular dean felt *comfortable* with his faculty, staff, and students and became confident in his role in the university, his place in his profession as a dean, and his role as a leader in the academic community. At any time, critical events challenging the support of the college, the financial stability of the economy, the practice of the education profession, or mission of the college may interrupt and destroy this sense of calmness. At this point in the socialization process, a seasoned dean responds by learning and taking action, not as a newcomer but as an experienced administrator.

Re-engagement/Renewal

Once the intended inner changes have taken place, a person reenters the social order on a new level of the professional plateau (See Figure 2.1). Not all deans, however, successfully transcend the socialization process and resettle with a sense of reengagement. Some have difficulty and may choose not to settle in. Either they haven't learned, or they don't like, their new culture. Some academics reject their new administrative roles and wish to return to faculty status.

Table 2.7
Incorporation of the Dean Taking Charge and Settling In

Phases of Incorporation					
	Taking Hold	**Immersion**	**Reshaping**	**Consolidation**	**Refinement**
Primary Themes	Summer & Fall Semester	Spring Semester	Summer & Fall Semester	Spring Semester	
	• Appoint team • Transition plan • Orientation & introductions • Establish values, style, expectation • Evaluation • Networking • Active Learning • Corrective actions	• Personnel issues • Sense making • Establish work relations • Build leadership team • Routine learning • Learning routine • Budget development	• Personnel changes • Systemic actions – organization changes • University service • College image -- GASing	• Coalition building • Corrective action • University, College visibility	• New opportunities • Fine tune operation • Settling in
Dominant Leadership Style	Human Resources	Structural	Symbolic	Political	Situational
Psychological Orientation	Confusion	Commitment	Competence	Confidence/ Comfort	Control?

IMPLICATIONS

For many deans, this transition into leadership creates an entirely new life. While faculty enjoy stable careers, the transition to a deanship is a transition to a new profession. Some of the prices deans pay when they enter the deanship deal with time commitment and the pressure to find balance in their lives. The role of the dean gives an identity and self-concept that often dictates with whom deans socialize, where they live, how long they retain their position, and what lifestyle they lead. Obviously, being a dean plays an important part in their lives and provides them with pleasures as well as pressures. What price do deans pay for their venture into college leadership? Where will it lead? What are the benefits? What are the costs? What changes have occurred in their personal lives, and are they satisfied with these changes? These are some of the questions that will be explored in the subsequent chapters.

PART II

Dimensions—Duties and Challenges

CHAPTER 3

Dean Leadership

"Leadership is one of the most observed and least understood phenomena on earth" (Burns, 1978, p. 2). In institutions of higher education, even the development of leaders has received little attention (Astin & Astin, 2001). The literature, however, is replete with books, articles, and commentaries on leadership—increasing at an exponential rate over the past two decades. Two of the most prolific writers on leadership, Bennis and Nanus (1985), concluded, however, that "books on leadership are often as majestically useless as they are pretentious" and insisted that they did not want "to further muddle the bewildering melange of leadership definitions" (p. 20). The pages logged under the heading of leadership make the work almost impossible to track for scholars of leadership theory and incomprehensible for deans attempting to practice it.

In this chapter we do not attempt to recount theories or recite definitions. Instead, we provide an overview of leadership, propose a definition of academic leadership, and assess the degree to which deans exhibit the behaviors embedded in academic leadership.

OVERVIEW OF LEADERSHIP

The problem with most approaches to leadership is that they have emphasized what is (a) *peripheral* to the nature of leadership and are (b) limited to the *content* of leadership in particular professions (Rost, 1993). Over the decades, traditional leadership scholars and theories have been predominantly focused on the *peripheries* of leadership: traits, personality characteristics, goal attainment, effectiveness, contingencies, situations, and style. On the *content* level, they emphasize what leaders need to know about a particular profession or institution in order to influence it. The content of leading focuses on understanding human behavior, professional practices, environmental needs, future trends, and the latest leadership theories. The result: "leadership scholars have spilled much ink on the peripheral elements surrounding leadership and its content instead of on the nature of leadership as a process, on leadership viewed as a dynamic relationship . . . the process whereby leaders and followers relate to one another to achieve a purpose" (Rost, 1993, p. 4).

Scholars have also been biased by their disciplinary perspectives. Most of the people who call themselves leadership scholars study leadership in one academic discipline or profession: Bailey (1988) in anthropology, Bass (1985) in social psychology, Selznick (1957) in sociology, Sergiovanni (1990) in education, Birnbaum (1990) in higher education, Schein (1992) in organizational development, Tucker (1981) in political science, and Zaleznik (1989) and Kouzes and Posner (1993), along with a host of others, in business, writing primarily for corporate executives. In contrast, examples of multidiscipinary scholars who have written books on leadership are still somewhat rare. Of these, Burns (1978) is probably most widely read, but others who have significantly contributed to the interdisciplinary approach are Helgesen (1995), Gardner (1990), Greenleaf (1977), Maccoby (1981), Kellerman (1999), Heifetz (1994), Rost (1993), Wheatley (1992), Conger and Benjamin (1999) and Bennis (1999). Some, such as Peters and Waterman (1982), have developed a more generalized view of leadership that reaches across professions, although they are more noted for their studies of business leadership.

Since 1978, two rubrics have dominated the scholarly work on leadership: transactional and transformational (Burns, 1978). *Transformational* leaders are viewed as directing and having personal impact on their colleagues (followers) and are sought after as a source of motivation and inspiration. In contrast, *transactional* theory defines leadership as a reciprocal process of social exchange between leaders and followers. Bensimon, Neumann, and Birnbaum (1989) believe that even though the transformational perspective on leadership in higher education "enjoys rhetorical support, it is an approach that in many ways may not be compatible with the ethos, values, and organizational features of colleges and universities" (p. 74). They postulate that while transformational theory is seductive, transactional theory may be more characteristic of leadership on most campuses. Deans, as leaders, may in fact fall into either one of these camps or in both, where it may be a matter of degree rather than an either-or situation (Wolverton, Gmelch, Montez & Nies, 2001). Although the hierarchical structure, reward systems, and tenure and promotion processes favor a transactional approach to leadership, our study supports the view of deans as somewhat transformational as they work with their faculty and colleagues.

ACADEMIC LEADERSHIP DEFINED

Based on a synthesis of Burns's (1978) transactional and transformational leadership and other attempts at defining leadership (Gardner, 1987; Greenleaf, 1977; Rost, 1993), we posit academic leadership as *the act of building a community of scholars to set direction and achieve common purposes through the empowerment of faculty and staff*. This definition presupposes three conditions deans must meet if they are to effectively lead their colleges.

Building a Community of Scholars

Building a community of scholars means moving away from a more "autocratic" control of a collection of "independent" faculty members toward the collaborative leadership of a community of scholars (Wolverton, Gmelch, & Sorenson, 1998). The college becomes a community in which faculty not only are loyal and dedicated to their discipline but work equally for the cause of the college. Thus, the college becomes a place where faculty go beyond their disciplinary loyalties and view their colleges as academic homes—places of identification, support, camaraderie, and social responsibility (Pew Policy Perspectives, 1996).

In turn, deans involve others in new ideas and projects, support effective coordination by working cooperatively with others, and make faculty feel like part of the group or college. A sense of caring marks an environment in which deans are concerned about the feelings of others, treat others with respect, and communicate feelings as well as ideas. It is an interpersonal relationship that depends on multidimensional, noncoercive influences. These reciprocal influences are based on the ability of deans to establish a sense of community, a team of academics among and with faculty and staff, through their personal rather than positional power. Although such a team orientation is necessary, it is also clear that deans must take responsibility for moving their colleges forward toward a common purpose—thus the second condition of academic leadership.

Setting Direction

Understanding why we exist and what it is that we want to accomplish as a college does not automatically happen. Faculty do not necessarily wake up one morning and say to themselves, "Collectively, as a college, this is where we want to be in five years, and here's how we're going to get there." Faculty need to be actively involved in planning for the college's future, but deans must encourage, direct, and inspire their academic colleagues to move toward these common goals. In order to set direction, they must communicate a clear sense of priorities, encourage others to share their ideas of the future, collaborate with others in defining a vision, and be oriented toward action (transformational leadership) rather than the status quo (transactional leadership). Common purposes that define future direction cannot be realized, however, if faculty and staff are not empowered to achieve the desired results.

Empowering Others

Bennis (1999) points out that empowerment is the collective effect of leadership. Deans demonstrate empowerment by making faculty feel significant and part of the community, valuing learning and competence, engaging faculty in exciting work, providing the resources required to do a good job, making expectations clear, helping faculty get the knowledge and skills necessary to perform effectively, recognizing and rewarding faculty for effective performance, and sharing power and influence with others. In essence, academic leadership empowers others to effect change.

DEANS AS LEADERS

We believe that deans as leaders should be actively engaged in each of these three endeavors. To assess whether they exhibited the qualities reflected in our definition of academic leadership, we asked deans in our study to indicate the degree to which specific behaviors characterized their practice of leadership. Table 3.1 displays the eight-item scales, which approximate each of the three leadership dimensions—community building, setting direction, and empowering others.

Each dimension consists of eight items. Each item was rated on a 1 (low) to 5 (high) scale regarding to what extent each statement characterized their behavior. A composite score, ranging from 8 to 40, was calculated for each dimension. Figure 3.1 plots the average combined scores for all the deans on each of the three individual dimensions. Mean scores for each of the qualities of dean leadership were consistently high (33 to 34), with the

Table 3.1
Academic Leadership Defined

Building Community	Setting Direction	Empowering Others
I show I care about others. I show concern for the feelings of others. I involve others in new ideas and projects. I support effective coordination by working cooperatively with others. I communicate feelings as well as ideas. I treat others with respect regardless of position. I provide opportunities for people to share ideas and information. I make others feel a real part of the group or organization.	I communicate a clear sense of priorities. I encourage others to share their ideas of the future. I engage others to collaborate in defining a vision. I willingly put myself out front to advance group goals. I have plans that extend beyond the immediate future. I am oriented toward actions rather than maintaining the status quo. I consider how a specific plan of action might be extended to benefit others. I act on the basis that what I do will have an impact.	I make sure people have the resources they need to do a good job. I reward people fairly for their efforts. I provide information people need to effectively plan and do their work. I recognize and acknowledge good performance. I help people get the knowledge and skills they need to perform effectively. I express appreciation when people perform well. I make sure that people know what to expect in return for accomplishing goals. I share power and influence with others.

actual scores ranging from 21 to 40. These results may stem from the fact that all three dimensions were strongly correlated with their perceptions of leadership effectiveness, and the deans in the study, for the most part, believed that they were effective leaders. On average, they reported leadership effectiveness ratings of 4.1 and 4.2 on a 5-point scale for men and women, respectively. If, as we surmise, all three conditions are essential components of academic leadership and deans believed themselves to be good leaders, then it is not surprising that their ratings were strong and balanced across the dimensions.

In comparing subpopulations, some statistically significant differences were found (see Table 3.2). Female deans consistently scored higher than male deans on building community, empowering others, and setting direction. These findings are consistent with other research supporting the supposition that women tend to be more relational and transformational in their leadership style compared to men, who tend to favor a more competitive, transactional style (Helgesen, 1995). Minority status deans also scored significantly higher on these dimensions than did majority deans. However, the differences between men and women and minority and majority deans are not practically different enough (1 to 2 points on a 32-point scale) to suggest that we would observe differences in dean leadership behaviors.

Figure 3.1
Qualities of Dean Leadership

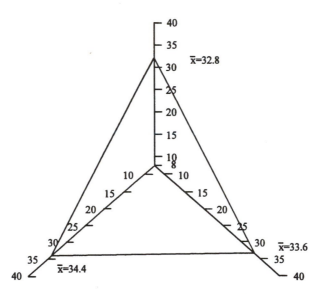

Community Building

Setting Direction   Empowering Others

The degree to which deans view themselves as administrators, as aca-demic faculty members, or as both also has a statistically significant impact on their perceptions of their leadership qualities. Deans who still see them-selves primarily as faculty members did not rate themselves as strongly on the dimension of setting direction for the college (mean score of 32) as those who saw themselves primarily as administrators (mean score of 34). Those who perceive themselves as both administrators and faculty mem-bers showed no significant difference on any of the dimensions of leader-ship qualities. If deans planned to return to faculty positions in the near future, they were less likely to engage in any of the three leadership dimen-sions than were other deans. A somewhat disconcerting finding suggests that some deans may overstay their welcome. Deans who had been in their positions for more than ten years were typically less likely to be enthusiastic about setting direction for their colleges. Perhaps over time deans become complacent, or they lose touch with the current realities of their colleges, or they believe that a direction set is a direction written in stone that re-quires no future revision, or maybe they simply get tired.

Table 3.2
Dean: Leadership Qualities

	Overall Mean (n = 749)	Men	Women	Minority	Majority
Building Community	34.4	33.8	35.2***	35.2**	34.3
Setting Direction	33.6	33.0	34.4***	34.4**	33.5
Empowering Others	32.8	32.3	33.5***	33.9**	32.7

**p-value ≥ .05
***p-value ≥ .001

To what extent does institutional culture or disciplinary orientation influence deans' leadership attributes? The only differences found among deans with regard to institutional type was in "community building," which appeared to be stronger in comprehensive universities and less prevalent among deans at research universities (Table 3.3). Given the nature of research universities, where cultivating independent scholars with aggressive personal research agendas is paramount to establishing a college's reputation, it seems reasonable that deans at research universities may be working more with a *collection* of scholars than with the *communities* of scholars we find at comprehensive universities. Again, these statistically significant differences represent tendencies, not necessarily practical differences.

Previous research on faculty suggests that many of their academic behaviors are discipline-specific. It appears that deans, socialized as faculty into different disciplinary cultures, also exhibit differences in their leadership attributes. When deans were compared across colleges, several statistically significant trends emerged (See Table 3.3). Education deans were significantly more engaged in the behaviors that contribute to each of the three attributes of building community, setting direction, and empowering others than were the deans of the other colleges. In contrast, business deans rated each of the three attributes as significantly less characteristic of their behavior as deans than did their counterparts in other colleges. This dichotomous observation leaves room for speculation and discussion about cultural differences between colleges of business and education. Liberal arts deans were less apt to set direction or to empower others. Setting direction seemed more characteristic of nursing deans than of other deans.

With regard to the deans' motivation to serve, those who were "other-oriented" (i.e., chose to be a dean in order to "contribute to and improve the college" or "influence the development of the faculty") favored

Table 3.3
Dean Leadership Qualities by Type of Institution and College

	Building Community	Setting Direction	Empowering Others
Type of Institution			
Research	33.9**	33.7	32.5
Comprehensive	34.7*	33.7	33.0
Baccalaureate	34.5	33.3	32.9
College (Discipline)			
Liberal Arts	34.4	32.8***	32.4**
Business	33.4***	33.1*	33.2**
Education	34.9**	34.2***	33.3**
Nursing	34.6	34.3***	33.2

*p-value ≥ .10
**p-value ≥ .05
***p-value ≥ .001

the leadership attributes of setting direction and empowering others more than did other deans. Finally, deans' perceptions of job satisfaction were moderately correlated with the attribute of empowering others.

IMPLICATIONS

Although most of the research has been aimed at understanding the peripheral aspects and content of leadership, our investigation of deans focused on understanding the essential nature of leading a college—the process whereby deans and faculty relate to one another through the dimensions of community building, setting direction, and empowerment. Indeed, deans were not found to be monolithic but were balanced in their approach to leadership.

Institutionally, deans in comprehensive universities described themselves more as community builders than did deans in research universities. As one might expect, it may be more difficult for deans to "herd cats" and get them to go in the same direction at research universities, where faculty expect a greater degree of freedom and autonomy (Bennis, 1999). As cultures vary in institutions of higher education, so might the requirements for and expectations of deans. The right job fit may be an important consideration for both deans and universities.

Previous studies of faculty have shown that such behaviors as stress, goal setting, and satisfaction vary according to disciplinary differences (Creswell, Wheeler, Seagren, Egly, & Beyer, 1990; Gmelch, Lovrich, & Wilke, 1984; McLaughlin, Montgomery, & Malpass, 1975). In contrast to faculty, academic leaders (department chairpersons and deans) across disciplines are more alike than different when compared by discipline (Gmelch & Burns, 1994; Gmelch, Wolverton, Wolverton, & Sarros, 1999; Wolverton, Wolverton, & Gmelch, 1999). Nevertheless, in this study, education deans reported statistically stronger leadership behavior in setting direction, empowering others, and building community than did deans from other colleges. Although the absolute differences in their scores reported in Table 3.2 may not result in differences in leadership styles, they do reflect the potential influence of the deans' disciplinary backgrounds on their approach to leadership.

Finally, it appears that years in the position take their toll on deans. If the challenges of the position continue to expand and become more complex, the tenth year in a dean's career may prove to be a turning point of sorts. After this juncture, deans seem to disengage from an activity, direction setting, that could prove crucial to the well-being of their colleges. Such disenfranchisement may simply indicate the need for a change in their careers—a move back to faculty or into another type of administrative position.

CHAPTER 4

What Deans Do

In college deans, we see a subtle shift in perception. Unlike department chairpersons, who in general view the activities in which they engage as a set of tasks to be completed, deans think in terms of roles and responsibilities. Roles are contextual. That is, they are associated with a specific set of people who function within a particular environment (Hewitt, 1997; Woods, 1992). Behaviors related to these roles derive from expectations, whether self-imposed, institutionally imposed, or externally driven. A dean's general experience, knowledge, values, perceptions, and institutional-specific encounters meld together with the demands of external constituents to determine what deans do (Rizzo et al., 1970). For example, a college dean who remains an active researcher does so because faculty, central administrators, or both expect him or her to do so. Deans who serve as institutional lobbyists respond to different expectations held by other constituency groups.

Quite often, people with a specific identity engage in similar roles because those behaviors are expected of them. For instance, department chairpersons act as advocates for faculty within their departments, whereas college deans champion their colleges as whole entities. Consequently, if a person aspires to a certain identity, the requisite roles must be learned and the prescribed patterns of behavior must become characteristic of the aspirant (Bates, 1956; Biddle, 1979; Levy, 1952). Another way to say this is that roles are what people do as occupants of a position (Newcomb, 1950).

People within the position can be differentiated from those in other types of positions on the basis of commonly held attributes and behaviors and the similarity in the way others respond to them (Biddle & Thomas, 1966).

For deans, such commonalities have changed over time. At the inception of the deanship in the United States in the 1800s, scholar-deans did little more than provide emotional support to students (McGrath, 1936, 1999). The responsibilities of deans, however, rapidly expanded to include such tasks as student discipline, admissions, supervision of faculty, and oversight of instruction (Dibden, 1968; DuPont, 1968; Griffiths & McCarty, 1980). With control over these crucial university endeavors, college deans became chief advisors to university presidents (Dibden, 1968).

Before 1950, universities were relatively small, and deans could be all things to all people. However, in the latter half of the twentieth century, as colleges and universities grew in size and complexity, the roles associated with the deanship gravitated away from a student service focus and toward an administrative one. Rapid expansion in the 1960s brought with it new positions, such as registrar, dean of students, and admission officer, momentarily leaving deans with the false impression that they could again return to being scholar deans (Dill, 1980; Dupont, 1968). In the late 1970s, most deans claimed a role in intellectual leadership, but few identified organizing activities within the college, staff development, public relations, program development, or budgetary activities as primary responsibilities (Cyphert & Zimpher, 1980). By the 1990s, deans described themselves as personnel managers, cultural representatives, communicators, financial planners, and advocates (Creswell & England, 1994; Martin, 1993; Twombly, 1992), and some admitted playing a critical role in college fund-raising efforts as well (Hall, 1993; Wisniewski, 1998). Evolution from academic dean to academic manager was underway (Tucker & Bryan, 1988).

WHAT DEANS DO TODAY

In today's colleges, six role sets define what deans do. Three of these role dimensions—fiscal resource management (Table 4.1), academic personnel management (Table 4.2), and internal productivity (Table 4.3)—clearly relate to management issues. Effective fiscal and academic personnel management guarantee that a college employs its resources in a manner that ensures effective daily operation and internal productivity. Deans agree that these three role sets are associated with the position. Specifically, fiscal resource management refers to keeping proper records and responsibly managing both nonacademic staff and fiscal resources. Fulfilling these re-

Table 4.1
Resource Management

Role Set Variables
Manage non-academic staff
Assure maintenance of accurate college records
Manage college resources (grants, facilities & equipment)
Keep current with technological changes
Comply with state, federal & certification agency guidelines
Variance accounted for: 4.7 %

Table 4.2
Academic Personnel Management

Role Set Variables
Recruit & select chairs & faculty
Evaluate chair & faculty performance
Supervise department chairs and directors
Variance accounted for: 4.0 %

sponsibilities helps to ensure that the college functions smoothly and effectively.

Academic personnel management encompasses recruiting, selecting, and evaluating chairpersons and faculty. It determines the strengths of the college in terms of programs offered and reputation garnered in the academic arena.

Internal productivity gets at the heart of operations—teaching, meeting the goals of the college, and realizing the mission of the university. A healthy work environment depends on effective and open communication. In it employees can grow professionally in and out of the classroom. Indeed, this third role set cannot be realized at its highest potential unless deans pay serious attention to fiscal and personnel management.

The remaining three role sets—scholarship (Table 4.4), leadership (Table 4.5), and external and political relations (Table 4.6)—are somewhat more contentious. Much of the common variance in the data is explained by these three dimensions, suggesting that many deans are still trying to decide exactly what their roles are. However, their presence does imply an understanding of the deanship as more than mere management and a recognition of the position's complexities and the need to lead.

Personal scholarship and dealing with leadership responsibilities accounted for slightly higher percentages of the data's variability than did the three operational role sets. In each case, the variability reflected in these

Table 4.3
Internal Productivity

Role Set Variables
Maintain effective communication across departments Communicate goals/mission to college employees/constituents Foster good teaching Maintain conducive work climate Encourage faculty, chair & staff professional development activities Participate in college/university committee work
Variance accounted for: 4.2 %

Table 4.4
Personal Scholarship

Role Set Variables
Maintain my own scholarship program & associated professional activities Remain current with my own academic discipline Demonstrate/model scholarship by publishing/presenting papers regularly Maintain & foster my own professional growth
Variance accounted for: 8.2 %

dimensions indicates some disagreement among deans in the study as to the importance of these roles. Maintaining a personal scholarship agenda, keeping current in one's discipline, and demonstrating and modeling scholarship, the three fundamental aspects of the personal scholarship dimension, are dean-specific. The extent to which deans engage in these roles determines how closely they relate to their peers professionally.

The variables that underlie the leadership dimension are college-specific. Informing college employees of university and community concerns, soliciting ideas to improve the college, assigning work, and planning and conducting college leadership meetings are duties that help to position the college within a broader context.

Clearly, the most controversial part of the deans' jobs revolves around the roles captured by the external and political relations dimension. Almost 25 percent of the variance in the data is accounted for by this factor. The variables that constitute this role set point to contextual issues. Funding, financial planning, building constituency involvement, promoting diversity, and ensuring alumni support, coupled with the political realities of representing one's college to the administration, all require that deans interface with groups outside the college and, in many instances, peripheral to the university. The two themes reflected in this role set distance

Table 4.5
Leadership

Role Set Variables
Inform college employees of university & community concerns Solicit ideas to improve the college Assign duties to chairs & directors Plan & conduct college leadership team meetings Coordinate college activities with constituents Represent college at professional meetings
Variance accounted for: 6.1 %

Table 4.6
External and Political Relations

Role Set Variables
Build relationships with external community/stakeholders Obtain & manage external funds (grants, contracts, donations) Foster alumni relations Develop & initiate long range college goals Financial planning, budget preparation & decision making Foster gender & ethnic diversity in the college Represent college to the administration
Variance accounted for: 23.5 %

deans from their more traditional faculty-related, operational roles and move them into two arenas that lie outside the immediacy of the college. The first, external relations, requires that deans relate to and work with constituencies outside the university. For instance, deans must build constituency involvement, seek external funding, and foster alumni relations. The second subset takes deans outside the college environment but keeps them within the context of the university. Here they must represent their colleges to central administration and engage in long-range planning and budgeting so that their colleges can gain the university support needed to operate effectively.

How Important Are These Roles?

This latter fundamental role set may be the most controversial because deans do not see it as one of their primary responsibilities. Although they view it as more important than some of their other roles, they may see it as a time-consuming distraction from what they believe is their "real" job—ensuring internal productivity through effective academic and fiscal management.

When the six role sets are ranked by mean score (Table 4.7), the relative positioning of them indicates the importance placed on them by deans in the study. Internal productivity ($\bar{x}$ = 4.37, on a 5–point scale with 5 high) and academic personnel management ($\bar{x}$ = 4.27) surface as the first and second concerns, followed closely by external and political relations ($\bar{x}$ = 4.16). The relatively small standard deviations in the case of the academic personnel management (s.d. = 0.59), internal productivity (s.d. = 0.43), and external and political relations (s.d. = 0.56) dimensions again suggest a fair amount of agreement among deans about the primacy of these roles. In contrast, personal scholarship, the dimension that explains the second largest proportion of variance in the data, ranked last in importance, with a mean score of 3.52. The fact that dealing with the external and political realities of the position ranks third is perhaps a grudging recognition of reality. Without support from university administration and external constituents, colleges find it difficult to realize their missions.

If we examine the six role sets in terms of the percentages of respondents who rated a role as highly important (5), we gain an even clearer picture. Academic personnel management was rated 5 by 19 percent of respondents and internal productivity by 10 percent. Opinion wanes significantly on whether external and political relations (4.4 percent), leadership (2.6 percent), scholarship (6.6 percent), and resource management (2.4 percent) are or should be high priorities. The relatively low mean score of this last dimension, resource management, may indicate that although deans see this as a dimension of the deanship, it may be a delegated one. They may ultimately be held responsible for the efficient use of available resources, but engaging in the specific actions associated with this charge may fall to someone else—a budget officer, for instance. Even though some deans rated ex-

Table 4.7
Relative Importance of Role Sets

Role Set	Mean	St. Dev.	Min.	Max.	% Rating 5
Internal Productivity	4.37	0.43	3.00	5.00	10.2%
Academic Personnel Management	4.27	0.59	1.00	5.00	19.4%
External & Political Relations	4.16	0.56	2.29	5.00	4.4%
Leadership	3.76	0.66	1.33	5.00	2.6%
Resource Management	3.62	0.68	1.60	5.00	2.1%
Personal Scholarship	3.52	0.87	1.00	5.00	6.6%

ternal and political relations as highly important, most did not feel as strongly about this role set as they did about internal productivity and academic personnel management.

What Deans Think Gives Meaning to Their Roles

Sometimes opinion varies within a group of people, even though its members fill comparable positions. Deans are no exception. Table 4.8 displays a number of personal and institutional variables that seem to impact the importance deans place on each role set. Interestingly, little disagreement seems to exist about the importance of roles central to the college mission—internal productivity and academic personnel management—and few variables impact deans' perceptions of their importance.

In contrast, several personal and institutional variables seem to influence the most disputed dimension, external and political relations. This dimension represents the most recently assumed role set. The possibility exists that some deans resist (or perhaps resent the necessity of) engaging in activities such as fund-raising and lobbying with university administrators and state legislators or other benefactors for resources. They may equate the act of building strong external relationships with pandering to the every whim of an uninformed public. By the same token, deans may view planning and dealing with diversity when they have little control over revenue generation as central administration responsibilities, not their own.

Similarly, disagreement on the importance of personal scholarship seems to abound, and findings suggest that it could be age-related. Younger deans may naively believe that they can do it all—continue as scholars and be college administrators at the same time. Deans in midcareer may still function under the false hope of engaging in research at the level they did before taking the deanship. Deans over fifty-five years old may be reconciled to the fact that this is not going to happen, and instead they may turn their attention to making some other type of professional statement before retirement. Similarly, the disposition toward an administrative perspective seems to diminish the importance deans attach to personal scholarship.

To some extent, differences in focus (administrative versus faculty) also impact the importance of the leadership dimension. Deans who view themselves as administrators seem to have reprioritized their roles in favor of leadership (and engaging in the external and political aspects of the job) at the expense of personal scholarship. These deans, in fact, seem to consciously realign their own priorities to conform to those of central administration.

Likewise, the same sort of refocusing may occur with deans in urban institutions. In this case, the shift may take place naturally because constituency groups, private funding sources, and diverse populations are more readily available and accessible to deans at these universities than to deans who work in more remote locations. Such proximity may also make these groups more vocal and demanding because they "see and live with" the university every day. Deans at research and public universities are also highly interested in the external and political aspects of the position. Real or anticipated public funding cuts may in both instances drive this concern.

If deans were hired to bring about growth in their colleges, the leadership, personal scholarship, and resource-management dimensions took on greater importance. Here, strong leadership may be required to set direction and keep the college on the right path. In addition, if part of that growth includes increasing the college's visibility in terms of research and scholarly productivity, deans may feel compelled to serve as role models for their faculty. Likewise, anytime a college grows, whether in professional status within the academy or in numbers of students enrolled, the action consumes resources. Deans in such situations might understandably turn their attention to finding ways to efficiently and effectively use available resources.

Finally, women appear to take all roles more seriously than do their male counterparts. We might ask: Are women over-achievers, or simply afraid of being perceived as failures? The same can be asked about deans of color.

ROLE CONFLICT AND AMBIGUITY: FIGHTING INSTITUTIONAL SHADOWS

Early on, the devolution of power and responsibility was clear, from the president to the dean. With the advent of the modern university came a new breed of administrator, the provost, sandwiched in between the president and the dean, and deans became middle managers (Fagin, 1997). Deans today experience at least two types of "middleness." They have always occupied the nexus between central administration and faculty. However, as the president was replaced by a management team and sophisticated, hierarchical layers of authority, deans became advisors not to presidents but to provosts. The direct line of power from president to dean was, if not broken, significantly altered. Deans became buried deep within an ever evolving bureaucracy—leaders of professional bureaucracies (colleges) within professional bureaucracies (universities) (Mintzberg, 1983).

Table 4.8
Influences on the Dean Role Sets*

Role Set	Adds to	Subtracts From
External & Political Relations	Being female Being minority Hired for growth Hired for change View self as administrator Urban location Public institution Research university	Expect to return to faculty Hired to deal with crisis Hired to sustain programs
Personal Scholarship	Being female Being minority ≤ 55 years old View self as faculty & administrator	View self as administrator Public institution Research university
Leadership	Being female Hired for growth View self as administrator Urban location	View self as faculty Expect to return to faculty Hired to sustain programs Hired because willing Research university
Resource Management	Being female Being minority Hired for growth	Expect to return to faculty Hired to deal with crisis Hired because willing Research university
Internal Productivity	Being female Being minority	Expect to return to faculty
Academic Personnel Management	Being female	Expect to return to faculty Hired to deal with crisis

*Significant at $p \leq .10$

Tucker and Bryan (1988) described these new college deans as doves of peace intervening among warring factions, dragons holding internal and external threats at bay, and diplomats guiding and encouraging people who live and work in the college. Each role—dove, dragon, or diplomat—is rife with the possibility of conflicting expectations and ambiguous interpretations. As administrators in hierarchical settings, deans behave in ways that seem situationally appropriate to them, given the demands and expectations of those with whom they work (Getzels, 1952; Sargent, 1951). For example, a dean bargaining with a provost over a spousal accommodation for a prospective employee finds him or herself in a different type of situation than when dealing with faculty and departments battling over office assignments and space allocation. The social behavior employed by a dean might lean toward persuasion in the first instance and negotiation and arbitration in the second.

When expectations of the university run counter to those of the faculty, or when expectations of either entity remain ill defined, deans attempting to meet these expectations experience a certain amount of disequilibrium. For instance, central administration may direct deans to cut costs, an ambiguous assignment at best; faculty may want deans to spend more on travel, research support, and equipment, a desire that is in direct conflict with the university's edict of fiscal restraint. Thus the dean faces a no-win situation.

Deans are often confronted with situations that require them to play roles that conflict with their value systems or with each other. In a sense, they face the dilemma of trying to serve two masters: a faculty who wants the dean to remain inwardly focused on the everyday workings of the college and a provost who asks deans to assume duties external to the college. On the one hand, deans may be asked to provide personal support for department chairpersons, and on the other hand, they may be required to evaluate them. This constitutes role conflict.

Role ambiguity relates to the degree to which we have sufficient information with which to perform the task, or to ambiguous and problematic work requirements and performance expectations (Carroll, 1974; Gross, Mason, & McEachern, 1958; Kahn et al., 1964; Merton, 1957; Rizzo et al., 1970). When universities charge their deans with the responsibility of cutting 3 percent from their budgets with an additional 2 percent reversion, both of which follow three previous years of trimming budgets 2% per annum, the task becomes ambiguous, potentially arbitrary, and perhaps impossible to carry out. Early research specific to university administration indicated that role conflict and ambiguity problems permeate universities. Deans, especially, must weigh central administration expectations against those of college departments (Baldridge, 1971). In essence, role conflict and role ambiguity cast shadows over the deanship from which deans must free themselves as much as possible if they are to lead their colleges effectively.

Deans and Role Conflict and Role Ambiguity

When it comes to role conflict and role ambiguity (Table 4.9), deans in the study were clearest about what their responsibilities are ($\bar{x}$ = 5.51 on a 7-point scale, where 1 signifies "not true of my job" and 7 suggests "extremely true of my job"). They seem fairly certain about how much authority they have ($\bar{x}$ = 4.99); they appear to know exactly what is expected of them ($\bar{x}$ = 4.67); and "the explanation regarding what has to be done is clear" ($\bar{x}$ = 4.66). When asked about areas where role conflict could occur, working with two or more groups that operate differently seemed to cause the most problems ($\overline{x}$ = 4.72), followed by doing things that are apt to be accepted by one person and not accepted by others ($\overline{x}$ = 4.38) and receiving assignments without the proper resources and materials to execute them ($\overline{x}$ = 4.15) or without proper staffing ($\overline{x}$ = 4.14). However, the situation is not so simple. Who a dean is and what constitutes the university where he or she works can either compound or ameliorate role conflict and role ambiguity.

How Individual Differences Affect Perceptions of Role Conflict and Role Ambiguity

Researchers often point to gender as a source of difference in approaches to leadership, communication styles, and methods of decision making (Astin & Leland, 1991; Helgesen, 1990, 1995; Jamieson, 1995; Tannen, 1990, 1994; Tinley, 1994), yet responses from the deans we polled indicate no sig-

Table 4.9
Role Conflict and Ambiguity Responses

(descending order by mean response reflecting the extent to which statement is true of job)

Variable	Mean
Role Conflict	
I work with two or more groups who operate quite differently	4.72
I do things that are apt to be accepted by one person and not accepted by others	4.38
I receive an assignment without the proper resources and materials to execute it	4.15
I receive an assignment without the proper staffing to complete it	4.14
I have to do things that should be done differently	4.05
I have to work on unnecessary things	3.97
I receive incompatible requests from two or more people	3.73
I have to buck a rule or policy in order to carry out an assignment	3.53
Role Ambiguity*	
I know what my responsibilities are	5.51
I feel certain about how much authority I have	4.99
I know exactly what is expected of me	4.67
Explanation is clear regarding what has to be done	4.66
Clear planned goals exist for my job	4.38
I know that I have divided my time properly	4.36

*These items were reverse scored for analysis.
The Likert Scale used a range from 1 (low) to 7 (high).

nificant differences in the degree to which men and women experience role conflict and role ambiguity. Because our sample reflects a good gender mix (59 percent male, 41 percent female), this finding suggests that when deans discover ways to cope with or lessen role conflict and role ambiguity, the methods may be similar for both men and women.

Interestingly, while gender-based differences did not exist, some variance related to minority status did surface. Two plausible reasons come to mind that could explain why minority status deans experience less role ambiguity: purpose and preparation. In the first instance, these deans may come into the job with a set agenda. They may have been hired to bring diversity to the college in terms of students, faculty, staff, and overall organizational climate. In the second, it is possible that these deans, like many women, tend to overprepare for the position to which they aspire. They become better at what they do than others so that they will be taken seriously. These findings seem to imply that we may be able to learn how to reduce or deal with role ambiguity by more closely examining the experiences of minority-status deans.

Another important study result revolves around the issue of marital status. Role conflict and role ambiguity did not vary by marital status. If, however, a dean (married or not) had children living at home, both role conflict and role ambiguity increased significantly. Single parents seemed especially at risk of experiencing greater role ambiguity. The implications here seem fairly straightforward. Deans with children living at home suffer divided loyalties, most likely brought on by one of the few factors over which they have little control: time. They simply cannot be in two places at once—at work, in a meeting, at home, at a school conference, at a high school football game or soccer match, at a piano recital or a spelling bee, or at home when a child comes through the door at the end of a busy school day eager to talk to Mom or Dad. The lessons to be learned are twofold. First, prospective deans should be made aware of the difficulties they will face as they attempt to balance their personal and professional lives. Second, colleges and universities can take proactive stances that allow deans more flexibility in the way work gets done and the manner in which office hours are covered. They can also support deans with children at home by providing viable options for child care or child-care leave.

Deans in this study under fifty years of age, in general, suffered more role conflict and role ambiguity than older deans. Although findings did not suggest that this group of deans was significantly more likely to have children living at home, one has to wonder whether this type of pressure contributed to the conflict experienced by some younger deans. It may suggest that some amount of maturity and experience may equip deans to better cope with role ambiguity and conflict. It could also simply indicate that the younger deans are still getting acclimated to the notion of balancing administration and faculty expectations, of giving the proper weight to each group's concerns. Ironically though, deans who have served for two or more years encounter more role conflict. This prompts us to believe that deans and their colleges go through a honeymoon period that appears to be over by the second year, when vested interests among competing factions begin to assert themselves.

Whether deans consider themselves to be faculty, administrators, or a combination of the two reveals another telling bit of information. Clearly, those who describe themselves as both administrators and faculty are worse off than the other two groups. Although these deans do not exhibit any higher levels of role conflict, they do experience higher levels of role ambiguity. Trying to be all things to all people may compound role ambiguity for these deans. Those who view themselves as faculty experience less role conflict, probably because they have a good sense of what they will and will not do. They do, however, experience more role ambiguity, probably because some constituents do not agree with the dean's assessment of his or her role and consequently place demands on the dean that he or she finds unacceptable. In contrast, deans who see themselves as administrators experience normal levels of role conflict and far less role ambiguity. These deans may be more decisive and commanding or may simply be able to deal with ambiguity better than some of their counterparts. Unlike department chairpersons, who often look at their positions as temporary departures from their role as faculty, deans have made a conscious career move into administration. It is possible that deans have discovered what sacrifices have to be made and are willing to make them. For instance, they may be unable to engage in scholarly work to the degree previously experienced, but they may accept that as a condition of the deanship. This predisposition toward administration may also lessen ambiguity levels.

Finally, mentors seem to have a viable place in the work lives of deans. It appears that mentors can help new deans to define their responsibilities, set priorities and goals, delineate how much authority they actually have, and manage time effectively, thereby reducing role ambiguity. Table 4.10 shows personal influences on role conflict and role ambiguity.

How Institutions Affect Role Ambiguity and Role Conflict

The degree to which deans across different institutional classifications experience role conflict may be indicative of the current state of affairs in these institutions (Table 4.11). Deans at both research and baccalaureate universities appear not to encounter any higher levels of role conflict than

Table 4.10
Personal Influences on Role Conflict and Role Ambiguity

	Adds to	Subtracts from
Role Conflict	Children at home < 50 years old	View self as faculty Satisfied with personal scholarship
Role Ambiguity	Children at home View self as faculty View self as faculty & administrator	Minority status > 50 years old Had mentor View self as administrator Satisfied with personal scholarship

Table 4.11
Institutional Influences on Role Conflict and Role Ambiguity

	Adds to	Subtracts from
Role Conflict	Being at a comprehensive institution Business College dean Urban location Large faculty & staff Hired to bring about change	Being at a baccalaureate institution Nursing College dean See university as good place to work
Role Ambiguity	Liberal Arts College dean	Nursing College dean Hired to deal with growth See university as good place to work

do deans at other universities. In fact, deans at baccalaureate universities function with less role conflict, possibly because the mission of these institutions is clear and less complex—they are teaching institutions. Deans at comprehensive universities, however, experience much more role conflict. This may occur because these institutions occupy an uneasy middle ground. They are no longer purely teaching universities, and they are not doctoral degree–granting institutions but may have aspirations to be such. Deans, as a consequence, may face faculty predisposed toward teaching and at the same time central administrators focused on the potential fiscal resources and prestige that research can generate.

In a similar manner, business college deans may face conflicting demands: a faculty that prefers to function as it always has, an external constituency that demands more work-related course content and greater accountability, and students who want better and more convenient delivery systems. These deans may also experience higher levels of role conflict because they have more opportunities to engage in external consulting. To do so adds another set of expectations, which are at odds with the expectations imposed on them by both central administration and faculty. Likewise, the current debate that pits lifelong learning advocates against work-skill proponents may help to explain why deans of liberal arts colleges seem to experience more role ambiguity. They may not know exactly what is expected of them and their faculty and, consequently, may not be able to plan effectively. In addition, moves toward skill-based curricula may create philosophical dilemmas for both deans and their faculties. In contrast, deans of health-related colleges appear to experience much less ambiguity than their counterparts, suggesting that they understand what is expected of them. Clearly delineated professional standards that college graduates must meet to become certified in their field of study may quell many of the questions that might otherwise arise concerning what is expected of a nursing college and its people. In addition, many of these deans are women, and while in general gender was not a deciding factor in determining role ambiguity levels, the combination of this particular field and gender could have some impact.

The final institutional factor worth noting is reason for hire. Deans were given the following choices and asked to select one:

- I was best suited to deal with the growth of the college or university.
- I was best suited to facilitate change.
- I was best suited to deal with a crisis (financial, academic, staff, or other) in the college.
- I understood the college's programs and was dedicated to sustaining them.
- I was willing to serve as interim dean.

Whether a dean had been willing to serve as interim or had been brought in to deal with a crisis did not significantly impact role conflict or role ambiguity, perhaps because the former instance was deemed irrelevant and the latter clearly meant that there was only one course of action because the college's survival was threatened. The other three reasons for hire in some way defined the level of role conflict and role ambiguity that deans exhibited. Dealing with growth may have been less ambiguous because the college had an agreed-upon agenda. Sustaining current programs could have brought less role conflict into the system for a similar reason: people were in agreement about the college's direction. Bringing about change may have resulted in more role conflict, again for a related reason: people more than likely had different agendas. Lack of proper resources also often serves as a compounding factor to change efforts.

Finally, college size, in terms of numbers of students and full-time faculty, does not seem important. Nor does the number of departments within a college. What does seem crucial, however, is the percentage of tenured faculty and the number of associate deans that serve the college. When the majority of the faculty is tenured, this group as a whole may become more vocal and demanding and less willing to bow to the desires of central administration. This situation definitely puts deans in the middle between two battling giants—neither one eager, in most cases, to back down. In terms of associate deans, it appears that interaction with direct subordinates raises the level of role conflict for a dean. This may stem from an inability or unwillingness on the part of deans to delegate responsibility effectively, or it may result because the parties involved have not developed their communication and interpersonal skills to the extent necessary.

Role Sets, Role Conflict, Role Ambiguity: What Makes Deans Tick?

Deans have an understanding of the importance of each of the six role sets: academic personnel management, internal productivity, resource management, leadership, personal scholarship, and external and political relations. They also experience role conflict and role ambiguity. The question we might ask is: What is the relationship between each role set and role conflict and role ambiguity, respectively?

Table 4.12 details these relationships in a correlation matrix. Both the external and political relations and personal scholarship role dimensions are correlated with role conflict, positively in the first instance and negatively in the second. As role conflict increases, the importance of the external and political relations dimension appears to increase. This may suggest that if role conflict exists, deans find it easier to concentrate on activities, such as generating support for the college and fund-raising. By the same token, as role conflict increases, the importance of pursuing one's own research and writing decreases, indicating that perhaps deans, when forced to choose, really no longer see scholarship as part of the dean's job. A word of caution should be issued here, however. While the p-values are significant, they are not highly significant, and the correlation coefficients are quite small, which means that the coefficients of determination are minuscule. As a consequence, no causality can be assumed, and in fact we might conclude that each relationship is a spurious one with little or no meaning. (Role conflict and each of the remaining dimensions do not seem to be directly correlated.)

A more interesting insight can be drawn from the effect that role ambiguity appears to have on all six role dimensions. In each case, the correla-

Table 4.12
Correlation Coefficients between Role Conflict and Six Role Dimensions
and Role Ambiguity and Six Role Sets

	Role Conflict	Role Ambiguity
External/Political	0.095*	-0.166*
Personal Scholarship	-0.096*	-0.081*
Leadership	-0.001	-0.171*
Resource Management	-0.010	-0.080*
Internal Productivity	-0.050	-0.102*
Academic Personnel Management	0.014	-0.112*

*Significant at $p \leq .05$ or better

tion is either moderately or highly significant and negative. The conclusion here: when role ambiguity is present, deans have difficulty determining the roles in which they should engage at any one given time.

IMPLICATIONS

Deans define their roles along six dimensions—external and political relations, personal scholarship, leadership, resource management, internal productivity, and academic personnel management. These dimensions vary in importance, with internal productivity and academic personnel management ranking somewhat more crucial than the other four roles. Deans also experience role conflict and role ambiguity. Role ambiguity in particular may prove troublesome. Ill-defined responsibilities, mixed messages as to how much authority deans actually have, unclear or unstated expectations and goals, and a lack of clarity about what is to be done and how much time should be spent doing it leave deans in a kind of leadership limbo. In effect, universities may be setting deans up to fail.

In a world where deans come and go on a fairly regular basis (O'Reilly, 1994), role conflict and role ambiguity take their toll on job satisfaction, stress, effectiveness, and commitment (Fried & Tiegs, 1995; Kahn et al., 1964; Schaubroeck, Cotton, & Jennings, 1989). Universities and their deans can ill afford to ignore these effects. The results—high turnover, burnout, and low productivity—cost too much in terms of people, time, and money. Because deans provide a critical link in the academic decision-making process, universities (and deans themselves) must find ways to keep them at their peak.

CHAPTER 5

Work-Related Stress in Deans

Optimal levels of stress can energize deans, leading to greater productivity, enjoyment of what they do, and creativity (Cox & Harquail, 1991; Gattiker & Larwood, 1990; Tharenou, Latimer, & Conway, 1984). The end result of stress optimization is the ability to balance administrative and academic pressures and a dean's personal and professional lives. This chapter examines dean stress as a phenomenon in and of itself, and as it relates to person-environment fit and job satisfaction.

STRESS

Generally, stress has been distinguished by three basic orientations: systemic or physiological (e.g., Cannon, 1939; Selye, 1974), psychological (e.,g., Lazarus, 1966; McGrath, 1976), and social (e.g., Levine & Scotch, 1970). Many stress models build off the one first conceived by McGrath. This model explained stress as a four-stage, closed-loop process beginning with situations in the environment (A), which are then perceived by the individual (B), to which the individual selects a response (C), restating in consequences (D) for both the individual and the situation, which closes the loop. Each of the four stages is connected by the linking processes of cognitive appraisal, decision, performance, and outcome. The Managerial Stress Model (Gmelch, 1989) builds on McGrath's four-stage process but provides a broader perspective and clearer understanding of stress from a managerial perspective.

The Managerial Stress Model includes four primary components, or stages. The steps are set in sequential order and reflect a direct causal effect so that the variables in the first stage are hypothesized to be a direct cause of the variables in the second stage, and so forth. For example, the objective stressors (stage 1) in an organization's environment impact the perception of stress in the second stage. The degree to which an individual perceives stress from the external environment is influenced by a person's disposition and background characteristics.

Stage 1: Demands or Stressors

The process begins with a set of demands or stressors, which are both internal and external to the dean's work environment. McGrath postulated six categories: (1) task-based stress, (2) role-based stress, (3) stress intrinsic to the behavioral setting, (4) stress arising from the physical setting, (5) stress arising from the social environment, and (6) stress within the person system (1976, p. 1369). An early study of university faculty revealed five distinct dimensions of perceived stress: reward and recognition, time constraints, departmental influences, professional identity, and student interaction (Gmelch, Wilke & Lovrich, 1986). Recent studies of department chairs identified administrative tasks, academic role, administrative role, human relations, and external time as key dimensions of stress (Wolverton, Gmelch, Wolverton & Sarros, 1999). While each profession should be recognized for its unique demands and reflect its own multidimensionality in the stress construct, faculty, chairs, and deans share common dimensions of stress reflective of the academy and academic work, in general.

Stage 2: Perception of Stressors

Whether a demand or stressor produces a stress response depends on the perception of the individual. This stage was missing in previous stimulus-response models and unexplained in medical and behavioral approaches, which explored causal relationships between stressors and consequences. Stressors represent the objective environment, and the perception of the stressors is what psychologist (1948) Lewin called the "subjective" environment. According to Lazarus and DeLongis (1983), individuals appraise situations based on the degree to which they believe they will be harmed, threatened, or challenged. High perceivers of stress respond to a situation as a threat rather than a challenge. If a dean believes that a situation will require resources that he or she does not possess, he or she will respond differently than if resource problems do not exist. For example, if a dean perceives a confrontation with a student as not demanding excessive time or resources, stress will not ensue. In contrast, if another dean perceives the same confrontation as demanding resources of which he or she has little, a discrepancy exists, creating stress. Therefore, the situation may be perceived as a stressor by one dean and not by another.

Stage 3: Response to Perceived Stressors

A stress response results when a stressor is perceived as harmful, threatening, or challenging. Here, individuals' physiological and psychological responses are not end products of the stress process but methods of mediating the stressor prior to the consequences. Physiologically, an alarm is sent out without discrimination (nonspecific) to all organs of the body, producing a biochemical chain reaction. In such a reaction, the brain organizes the body for its response to stress by stimulating the hypothalamus, which adjusts the blood supply and relaxes the stomach, bladder, and intestines. The adrenal gland monitors the liver, pancreas, spleen, and large blood vessels and builds up the supply of fuel, whereas the thyroid gland increases energy production. This internal biochemical response translates into what experimental psychologists call an *orientation response*. The typical orientation response to such stress situations as public speaking might manifest itself in bodily reactions such as dilation of the pupils, increased heart rate, dry mouth, sweating palms, increased muscle tone, acute hearing, and changes in breathing patterns. Relatively few researchers have studied academic administrators' physiological reactions to stress (Cooper, Sieverding, & Muth, 1988; Phillipps & Thomas, 1983; Whan, 1988).

Although the physiological response is much the same for everyone, the psychological and behavioral reaction is a distinctly personal matter. Theorists postulate that psychological responses to stress can be categorized into four modes: (a) information seeking, (b) direct action, (c) inhibition of action, and (d) intrapsychic processes (Lazarus & Launier, 1978). In practice, these modes translate into coping categories: social, physical, intellectual, entertainment, personal, managerial, and attitudinal (Gmelch, 1989).

Stage 4: Consequences of Response

The fourth stage, consequences, differs from the responses because it takes into account the long-term effects of stress, both due to its duration and its intensity. The degree of stress perceived and actual stress may produce different problems in different individuals. At the extreme, if one is unable to alleviate some of the stressors or cope adequately, consequences may arise in the form of serious mental or physical illnesses. As Selye (1976) points out, the weakest link in the body breaks down first. A person's weakest link is idiosyncratic and may be determined through hereditary predispositions for heart disease, cancer, headaches, or depression. Therefore, each person has a different threshold to seemingly similar stressful situations. Some deans, by nature, will survive stress longer. Others have a low stress threshold and may succumb sooner. Figure 5.1 illustrates the four stages of the stress cycle.

DEAN STRESS

In the case of college deans, seven dimensions—administrative, provost-related, faculty or chairperson-related, time or personal, scholarship, salary or recognition, and fund-raising—surfaced. Administrative Task Stress (Table 5.1) encompasses variables that are very similar to the task-based stress items on instruments testing public school administrators and university department chairperson instruments. In all three cases, this dimension reflects the stress arising from the performance of administrators' day-to-day tasks and pressures of deadlines, meetings, paperwork, budgets, and interruptions.

Figure 5.1
Dean Stress Cycle

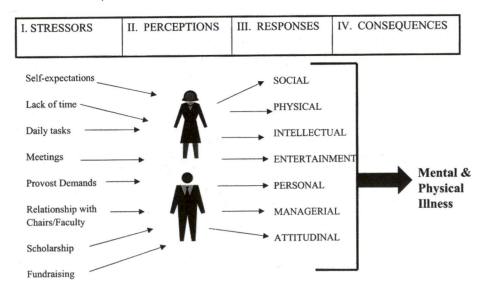

Source: Adapted from Walter H. Gmelch, *Coping with Faculty Stress* (Newbury Park, CA: Sage Publications, 1993).

Table 5.1
Variables Loading on Dean Administrative Task Stress

Meeting report and other paperwork deadlines*
Preparing budgets and allocating resources
Writing letters and memos, and responding to other paperwork
Feeling I have too heavy a work load*
Being frequently interrupted by telephone calls & drop-in visitors*
Attending meetings which take up too much time*
Having to make tenure, promotion & advancement decisions*

*Top rated stressors (*Imposing high self-expectations* was also a top stressor but was treated as unique). Cumulative percent of variance across all dimensions accounted for 59.9 (27.9% variance in the data by this dimension).

The Provost-Related (Table 5.2) and Faculty or Chairperson-Related (Table 5.3) Stress dimensions capture the role- and relationship-based conflict occurring between management levels. In the first instance, deans exhibit frustration with trying to resolve differences and conflicting demands with, and influence decisions of, their provost; having insufficient authority to perform their responsibilities; and feeling pressure for job performance without knowing how the provost evaluates their performance.

In the second instance, Faculty or Chairperson-Related Stress points to the conflict-ridden and personnel nature of academic administrator positions. This stress emanates from handing conflict with faculty and chairpersons as well as making staff evaluation and promotion and tenure decisions.

Time or Personal Stress (Table 5.4) represents a new dimension of administrator stress not previously identified. Although some of the items in this factor have appeared on other administrator stress instruments, this dimension of stress paints a more holistic picture of dean time demands, which stem from external, after-hour activities from social obligations, travel, and competition for time between the dean's personal and professional lives.

In contrast, Scholarship Stress (Table 5.5) in deans is similar to scholarship stress in department chairs. Deans express frustration from insufficient time to stay current in their academic field, not making progress in their academic career, and trying to balance their leadership and scholarship responsibilities. As with department chairperson stress, this dimension appears to be unique among academic administrators in higher education and is not found in public schools or business and industry.

Salary or Recognition Stress resembles one of the dimensions of stress expressed by faculty in an earlier study (Gmelch, Wilke, & Lovrich, 1986).

Table 5.2
Variables Loading on the Dean Provost-Related Stress

Resolving differences with my provost
Trying to influence the actions and decisions of my provost
Having insufficient authority to perform my college responsibilities
Feeling I will not be able to satisfy the conflicting demands of those in positions of authority over me
Feeling unreasonable pressure for better job performance
Not knowing how my provost evaluates my performance

Cumulative percent of variance across all dimensions accounted for 59.9 (8.4% variance in the data by this dimension).

Table 5.3
Variables Loading on the Dean Faculty or Chairperson Related Stress

Handling concerns and conflicts with faculty*
Handling concerns and conflicts with chairs
Evaluating chairs, faculty and staff performance
Having to make tenure, promotion and advancement decisions *

*Top rated stressors. Cumulative percent of variance across all dimensions accounted for 59.9 (6.1% variance in the data by this dimension).

This stress arises from the feeling of inadequate salary and insufficient recognition for administrative and scholarly performance.

Finally, Fund-Raising is the stress dimension most unique to deans and is most likely the newest dimension of dean stress. This dimension relates to current pressures on deans to engage in fund-raising and financial support activities and to satisfy demands of constituent groups.

JOB STRESS, PERSON-ENVIRONMENT FIT, AND JOB SATISFACTION

Deans in this study attributed 60 percent of the stress they experience to the job. Between 35 percent and 40 percent suggested that they work under excessive levels of stress. Critical dimensions of the work environment, unique characteristics of individuals asked to function within a given setting, and the fit between the person and the environment all impact work-related stress (Caplan, 1983; Caplan, Cobb, French, Van Harrison, & Pinneau, 1980; Dawis, England, & Lofquist, 1964; Holland, 1966; Kulik, Oldham, & Hackman, 1987). The fit (or lack of it) between deans and their colleges helps to determine whether they experience levels of stress

Table 5.4
Variables Loading on the Dean Time or Personal Stress

Participating in work-related activities outside regular working hours which conflict with personal activities
Meeting social obligations (clubs, parties, volunteer work) expected of deans
Having to travel to fulfill job expectations
Attempting to balance my professional and personal lives*

*Top rated stressor. Cumulative percent of variance across all dimensions accounted for 59.9 (5.2% variance in the data by this dimension).

Table 5.5
Variables Loading on the Dean Time Scholarship Stress

Having insufficient time to stay current in my academic field*
Attempting to balance my leadership and scholarship responsibilities*
Believing my academic career progress is not what it should be

*Top rated stressor. Cumulative percent of variance across all dimensions accounted for 59.9 (4.7% variance in the data by this dimension).

that move them forward in their work or suffer debilitating stress that leads to excessive physical and mental strain (Caplan, 1983; Caplan et al., 1980; Dawis, 1994; Dawis & Lofquist, 1984; Day & Bedeian, 1995). Further, research links person-environment fit, stress, and job satisfaction. The cumulative effect of these constructs enhances or detracts from overall work performance in deans (French & Caplan, 1972; Kahn, 1981; Kahn & Byosiere, 1992).

Personal Attributes

Several characteristics of deans influence the situation. For example, research literature suggests that as individuals age, they experience lower levels of work-related stress (Bergin & Solman, 1988). Researchers also agree that age has a positive effect overall on job satisfaction (Austin, 1985a; Clark & Oswald, 1996; Diener, Emmons, Larsen, & Griffin, 1985; Judge, Boudreau, & Bretz, 1994; Pfeffer & Langton, 1993; Sarros, Gmelch, & Tanewski, 1996). In other words, older deans should experience less job-related stress and be more satisfied in their positions.

Gender also seems to play a role in whether individuals exhibit excessive levels of stress and in how they define job satisfaction. Women consistently demonstrate higher levels of both job satisfaction and job-related stress (Austin, 1985b; Blix & Lee, 1991; Clark & Oswald, 1996; Holt,

Table 5.6
Variables Loading on the Dean Salary or Recognition Stress

Receiving inadequate salary
Receiving insufficient recognition for performing administrative functions
Receiving insufficient recognition for my scholarly performance

Cumulative percent of variance across all dimensions accounted for 59.9 (4.1% variance in
the data by this dimension).

Table 5.7
Variables Loading on the Dean Fund-Raising Stress

Having to engage in fund-raising activities
Trying to gain financial support for college programs*
Trying to satisfy constituent groups (e.g., alumni, legislators, community)

*Top rated stressor. Cumulative percent of variance across all dimensions accounted for
59.9 (3.6% variance in the data by this dimension).

1982; Karsten, 1994; Schonwetter, Bond, & Perry, 1993). Some research,
however, contradicts this job-satisfaction finding, suggesting that other issues, such as changing educational or institutional climates, may serve as
confounding variables. When race enters the equation, evidence points to
increased stress levels and decreased job satisfaction (Bartel, 1981; Brown,
1988; Graves, 1990; Sanders & Mellow, 1990; Tack & Patitu, 1992). Based
on previous research findings, female deans will most likely experience
high levels of stress but greater job satisfaction. Race may also play a role in
how well deans acclimate to their work environments.

Finally, experience contributes to job performance and success, two outcomes that interrelate with the variables—work-related stress and job satisfaction (Cox & Harquail, 1991; Gattiker & Larwood, 1990; Pfeffer &
Langton, 1993; Tharenou et al., 1994). Austin (1985a) found that years of
employment did not matter in terms of job satisfaction; what mattered was
the variety of skills the administrator could use in his or her work situation
and the type and amount of feedback received.

The Work Environment

In a similar fashion, research consistently demonstrates that institutional
variables can affect work-related stress, the person-environment fit, and
job satisfaction. The type of institution, discipline, prevailing practices and
expectations, and quality ratings of the institution and departments provide examples of both objective and subjective institutional factors that

impact person-environment fit, stress, and job satisfaction (Biglan, 1973; Bowditch & Buono, 1997; Caplan et al., 1980; Gmelch & Chan, 1994; Kuhn, 1970; Neumann & Boris, 1978).

For example, the more caring the environment, the more cooperative the climate, the more staff involvement in decision making, and the greater the perceived level of personal autonomy, the greater the level of job satisfaction will be (Austin, 1985a). Judge and Hulin (1993) found that perceived autonomy led to better mental health, an indicator of lower or optimal work-related stress levels. As for institutional size, research indicates that employees of smaller firms are happier (Clark & Oswald, 1996; Idson, 1990). Implied in this finding is the notion that smaller colleges and universities tend to be less complex and perhaps less stressful places to work, which enables deans to function with a greater degree of autonomy.

Other factors impact person-environment fit, stress, and job satisfaction as well. On-the-job role ambiguity and role conflict are major ingredients in the determination of levels of work-related stress and job satisfaction (Abdel-Halim, 1981; Bedeian & Armenakis, 1981; Fisher & Gitelson, 1983; Fried & Tiegs, 1995; Kahn et al., 1964; Rizzo et al., 1970; Sarros et al., 1996; Schaubroeck et al., 1989; Wolverton, Wolverton & Gmelch, 1999). Blix and Lee (1991) found that individuals in frontline managerial positions, such as the deanship, are more susceptible to work-related stress because they are caught between the controls from above and the demands from their former peer group. If they cannot cope adequately with this stress, they are more likely to consider changing jobs. If, in addition, administrators believe that they do not have the skills to perform the required work, this leads to lower levels of job satisfaction and reduced mental health, a potential outcome of excessive stress (Judge & Hulin, 1993). Self-imposed expectations also play a role here.

Recognition becomes important in the determination of job satisfaction. It results from the relationship between the effort an individual expends on the work and the recognition he or she receives in exchange. When the recognition received (either extrinsic or intrinsic) falls below the expected level, job satisfaction decreases and work-related stress may increase (Gupta & Beehr, 1979; Hulin, Roznowski, & Hachiya, 1985). In fact, one stream of research examines satisfaction with pay, a form of recognition, as a component of job satisfaction (Clark & Oswald, 1996; DeConinck, Stilwell, & Brock, 1996; Heneman & Schwab, 1985; McBride, Munday, & Tunnell, 1992; Summers & Hendrix, 1991). In most instances, equity variables, such as compensation schemes and work pace, were significant predictors of job satisfaction. If employees perceived that compensation was distributed fairly and that they were asked to complete work in a reasonable amount of time, job satisfaction increased (Bluedorn, 1982; Folger & Konovsky, 1989; Ronen, 1986; Scholl, Cooper, & McKenna, 1987). Austin (1985a), in her research on academic administrators, found that salary was a significant predictor of job satisfaction.

Academic organizations generate pressures and concerns that are peculiar to colleges and universities. In particular, academic administrators engage in a crucial balancing act between their leadership and administrative responsibilities and a desire to pursue their own scholarship. Stress results from attempting to strike this balance. This type of stress is directly related to job dissatisfaction and job stress (Booth, 1982; Lee, 1985; McLaughlin et al., 1975; Sarros et al., 1996). Deans also rate workload, frequent interruptions, and having to meet too many deadlines (which are work control issues) as top stressors. Furthermore, the way in which deans perceive their role confounds the situation (Kulik et al., 1987; Lazarus, 1979). Deans who see their role as being primarily administrative are impacted less by scholarship and work-control variables than are deans who view themselves as faculty members first and administrators second. Stress levels tend to be lower in the former. Funding for programs is also an important issue, as is faculty quality. The greater the need to secure funding for programs and the higher the quality of faculty, the higher the stress.

Finally, stress is not all bad. Indeed, we need stress; a complete lack of stress signals death (Quinn, Faerman, Thompson, & McGrath, 1990). Positive stress reflects itself in an individual's reactions to stressful situations. Stress at its best energizes, motivates, challenges, and helps individuals to concentrate. In work environments, desirable stress levels promote greater work effort, in part because they also stimulate awareness of options. Perceived success, rising to a challenge, taking advantage of an opportunity, and improving oneself are all positive stressors. In sum, ideal stress levels enhance performance, which in turn signifies a good person-environment fit and can lead to increased job satisfaction (Brewer, 1995; Gmelch & Chan, 1994; Ivancevich & Matteson, 1987; Lewis, Garcia, & Jobs, 1990).

INTERACTIONS BETWEEN SELECTED UNIQUE VARIABLES AND DEAN STRESS DIMENSIONS

The interrelatedness of many of these variables and the dean stress dimensions mirrors the image portrayed in previous research literature. For instance, Administrative Task (AT) Stress in deans increases significantly as self-imposed expectations rise, when role conflict exists, when promoting diversity and adapting to technological change are important, or when handling student conflict is part of the job description (Table 5.8). If deans view themselves as academics and have good working relations with faculty and students, stress increases. In general, women experience significantly higher levels of AT Stress. And, it appears that age and having children living at home may also have some impact. If, however, deans work at public institutions, research universities, or in business colleges, or have held the position for some time, this type of stress seems to be less.

When we examine the Provost Related (P) Stress dimension, role conflict, role ambiguity, and age adversely impact P Stress in deans (Table 5.4). Promoting diversity also increases P Stress levels. Deans who think of themselves as administrators, and deans of color, experience more of this type of stress. Those working in colleges of education or nursing experience less P Stress. A desire to improve the college also lessens P Stress.

Many variables seem to impact Faculty or Chairperson-Related (F/C) Stress (Table 5.10). Having to handle student conflicts, promoting diversity, and perceiving high student academic ability significantly increase F/C Stress. High self-expectations and viewing oneself as an administrator also add to this type of stress. The better the quality of relations between deans and their faculty and staff, and those between faculty and students, the lower the F/C Stress levels. Being female, minority, or older all appear

Table 5.8
Variables That Add to or Reduce Administrative Task Stress (AT)

Adds to	Reduces
High self-imposed expectations Role conflict Promoting diversity Adapting to technological change Handling student conflict Viewing self as an academic Good working relations with faculty & students Being female Having children at home	Being older Working at a public institution Working at a research university Working in a business college Years in position

Table 5.9
Variables That Add to or Reduce Provost-Related Stress (P)

Adds to	Reduces
Role conflict Role ambiguity Age Promoting diversity Minority status Viewing self as an administrator	Working in an education college Working in a nursing college Having a desire to improve the college

Table 5.10
Variables That Add to or Reduce Faculty/Chair-Related Stress (F/C)

Adds to	Reduces
High self-imposed expectations	Better quality relations with faculty & staff
Perceiving high student academic ability	Better relations between faculty & students
Promoting diversity	Being older
Handling student conflict	Being female
Viewing self as an administrator	Having minority status
Working at a public institution	Working in a business, education, or nursing college

Table 5.11
Variables That Add to or Reduce Time/Personal Stress (T/P)

Adds to	Reduces
High self-imposed expectations	Being older
High student ability	Viewing self as an academic
Works at a research university	Taking the position to advance career
Having children at home	Role ambiguity
Taking the position for power	
Role conflict	

to lower F/C Stress. The type of college also affects stress levels: working in a business, education, or nursing college seems to reduce F/C Stress. If deans work at public institutions, however, F/C Stress appears to increase.

Time or personal (T/P) Stress seems to lessen in deans as they age, if they think of themselves as faculty, or if they took the position to advance their academic careers (Table 5.11). It increases as self-imposed expectations increase, if the academic ability of students is deemed high, if the dean works at a research university, if children are living at home, or if a dean took the position for power. Role conflict increases T/P Stress; role ambiguity lowers it—perhaps because role conflict indicates that time-consuming duties are set and are competing for attention, whereas role ambiguity allows some flexibility in what gets done because expectations are not clearly defined.

Scholarship (S) Stress is significantly affected by the dean's overall satisfaction with personal scholarship levels (Table 5.12). The more satisfied the deans were, the less S Stress they experienced. In addition, deans who are older, in business colleges, perceive themselves as administrators, relate well to faculty and students, or have children living at home experience lower levels of S Stress. In the first instance, perhaps older deans are at a stage in their careers where their interests have moved away from research and publishing. Likewise, viewing oneself as an administrator may change the way in which deans define their work, downplaying research. In the case of deans with children at home, personal responsibilities may, in their minds, justify paying less attention to scholarship, thus reducing pressure to do it. Deans at public universities also experienced lower levels of S Stress. Adapting to technology adds to S Stress, perhaps because deans with limited amounts of time to devote to scholarship may find learning new technologies, which may or may not increase their scholarly production, frustrating.

Salary or Recognition (S/R) Stress for deans seems to be discipline-sensitive (Table 5.13). Business, education, and nursing deans experience increased stress in this area. In the first instance, this may occur because business deans can earn more in professional fields outside the academy. For deans in the other two colleges, it still may be a case of comparative worth, but the stress may stem from internal comparisons with deans in higher paying disciplines. Adapting to technological change adds to S/R Stress. In addition, several other variables appear to contribute to salary and recognition stress. These include the number of years as dean, the existence of role conflict and ambiguity, and dealing with student conflicts. If deans took the position either for financial gain or to advance their administrative careers, they also experience more stress. Promoting diversity decreases it, as does working with quality faculty.

Finally, Fund-Raising (FR) Stress is impacted by several institutional, personal, and work variables (Table 5.14). Adapting to technological change increase the levels of FR Stress. This may indicate that this responsibility comes as an unfunded, or minimally funded, mandate that forces deans to seek outside resources in order to move this agenda forward. Deans in public institutions experience more FR stress. This situation may be a relatively new development that has occurred as public funding for higher education has decreased. Deans experience more FR Stress when they are

Table 5.12
Variables That Add to or Reduce Scholarship Stress (S)

Adds to	Reduces
Adapting to technological change	Being older High satisfaction with level of personal scholarship View self as an administrator Working in a business college Relating well to faculty & students Having children at home Working at public universities

Table 5.13
Variables That Add to or Reduce Salary/Recognition Stress (S/R)

Adds to	Reduces
Years in position Role conflict Role ambiguity Working in a business, education, or nursing college Adapting to technological change Handling student conflict Taking position for financial gain Taking position to advance administrative career	Promoting diversity Working with quality faculty

Table 5.14
Variables That Add to or Reduce Fund-Raising Stress (FR)

Adds to	Reduces
High self-imposed expectations Role conflict Working at a public institution Adapting to technological change Handling student conflict Promoting diversity View self as an administrator Being satisfied with level of one's scholarly activity Being older Working at a research or comprehensive university Working in a nursing college	Years in position

charged with promoting diversity in the college. Age, viewing oneself as an administrator, and being satisfied with one's level of scholarly activity also adversely impact FR Stress; years in the position, however, lessen it. Deans at both comprehensive and research universities, as well as those in nursing colleges, experience significantly hi̇ ᴧer levels of FR Stress.

PERSON-ENVIRONMENT FIT AND DEAN STRESS

Person-environment fit and dean stress are interrelated. When deans and their colleges match, stress tends toward optimal levels. When a mismatch occurs, stress levels increase. Within this relationship, specific variables either exacerbate the lack of fit or contribute to situations where person-environment fit is better for deans.

For instance, in AT, P, F/C, T/P, and S Stress, the variables that significantly add to stress levels, for the most part, either define the dean or the work. The variables that significantly reduce stress are a combination of personal and institutional factors. Most striking is the realization that one or all of the work-defining variables (handling student concerns and conflicts, promoting diversity, and adapting to technology) show up as significant contributors to AT, P, F/C, and S Stress. Role conflict and role ambiguity, which could indirectly reflect student diversity and technology aspects of the job, increase AT, P, and T/P stress. AT and T/P Stress are primarily affected by personal variables—such as high personal expectations, having children at home, and motivation for taking the position—that lie somewhat within the control of the individual. The variables adding to these stress dimensions, which can be construed to be institutional in nature, deal with student academic ability and institutional type. They impact F/C and T/P Stress.

Personal variables dominate the list of stress-relieving influences across the AT, P, F/C, T/P, and S dimensions. Years as dean (AT Stress), desire to improve the college (P Stress), age, female status, minority status (F/C Stress) and the quality of the relations between dean and faculty (F/C Stress) appear to lower stress levels. The reason for taking the position also affects P and T/P Stress. Institutional variables that lead to lower levels of stress include being at a public institution (AT and S Stress), working at a research university (AT Stress), and being attached to professional colleges (AT, P, F/C, and S Stress).

Only in the S/R and FR Stress dimensions were institutional and work-defining variables dominant determinants of stress levels. S/R Stress and FR Stress were impacted by college type and by the work variable, adapting to technology. Role conflict and ambiguity (both work-related) and handling student conflicts also add to S/R Stress levels. Promoting diversity adversely affects FR Stress. The public status of institutions directly affects FR Stress (as do research and comprehensive designations), suggesting that deans in public universities must raise funds to support institutional priorities that change the nature of the dean's work. Interestingly, in both these types of stress, few variables mitigate stress levels, but those that do tend to be personal in nature. Years as a dean seem to make a difference. This may indicate that the longer deans are in their positions, the more comfortable they are with fund-raising, or perhaps the easier it becomes due to established relationships with constituents. The single variable positively affecting S/R Stress appears to be institution type. Deans at comprehensive universities experience lower levels of S/R Stress, suggesting that they may have lower salary expectations than deans at other types of universities. Promoting diversity also seems to lower S/R Stress. Table 5.15 summarizes these trends.

DEAN STRESS AND JOB SATISFACTION

Most research on job satisfaction and stress finds some relationship (either direct or indirect) between the two, and that relationship is usually reciprocal (Bateman & Strasser, 1983; Blau, 1981; Brooke, Russell, & Price, 1988; House, 1981; LaRocco, House, & French, 1980). In other words, when work-related stress exceeds optimal levels, job satisfaction declines and it compromises work outcomes, such as job performance, morale, and commitment to the organization (Assouline & Meir, 1987; Bedeian & Armenakis, 1981; Fried & Tiegs, 1995; Gupta & Beehr, 1979; Judge et al., 1994; Kahn & Byosiere, 1992; Matteson & Ivancevich, 1987; McGrath, 1976; Schwab, Jackson, & Schuler, 1986; Sutherland & Cooper, 1988). Likewise, the lack of job satisfaction, coupled with other exogenous influences, increases work-related stress. In higher education, Hagedorn (1996) found that the relationship was unidirectional. In a study of female faculty, she discovered that the level of job satisfaction directly impacted work-related stress but that stress levels did not affect whether these women were satisfied in their positions.

For deans in this study, a similar situation seems to hold true. Increased job satisfaction lowered the reported levels of work-related stress. In addition, age inversely influenced perceived stress levels, but having children who live at home increased it. In turn, dean job satisfaction was directly affected by several variables. For instance, female deans experienced lower job satisfaction. Increased role conflict and role ambiguity decreased job satisfaction. Organization size and adequate funding levels were positively related to job satisfaction. Each of these variables indirectly contributed to work-related stress through job satisfaction. Work-related stress did not appear to directly affect dean job satisfaction. Figure 5.2 sums up these findings.

IMPLICATIONS

Job satisfaction and person-environment fit are crucial determinants of the level of work-related stress experienced by deans. A lack of person-environment fit increases stress, as does low job satisfaction. Conversely, deans who experience high levels of job satisfaction may do so because they are in environments that they find conducive to work. This, in turn, in all likelihood leads to lower levels of work-related stress.

Table 5.15
Variables That Impact Person-Environment Fit by Stress Dimension

Variable	Increase							Decrease						
Personal Variables	AT	PS	FC	TP	S	SR	FR	AT	PS	FC	TP	S	SR	FR
Age		X					X	X		X	X	X		
Gender (Female)	X									X				
Children	X			X								X		
Years Dean						X		X						X
Minority Status		X								X				
Satisfied as Scholar						X						X		
Self Perception of Role as Faculty	X										X			
as Administrator		X	X			X					X			
as Faculty & Administrator														
Why Became a Dean														
Contribute to College									X					
Financial Gain						X								
Advance Adm. Career						X				X				
Power & Authority				X										
High Self-Expectations	X		X	X			X							
Relations with Faculty	X									X		X		
Institutional Variables														
Public			X			X		X				X		
Research			X			X		X						
Comprehensive						X								
Business						X		X		X		X		
Education						X			X	X				
Nursing						X	X		X	X				
Faculty/Student Relations										X				
Academic Quality of Students			X	X										
Quality of Faculty													X	
Work Variables														
Adapting Technology	X				X	X	X							
Promoting Diversity	X	X	X				X						X	
Handling Student Conflicts	X		X			X	X							
Role Conflict	X	X		X		X	X							
Role Ambiguity		X				X					X			

Figure 5.2
Tipping the Dean Stress Scales

- **Toward Excessive Stress Levels**
  - ➤ Having children at home
  - ➤ Being friends
  - ➤ Role conflict
  - ➤ Role ambiguity
  - ➤ Decreased levels of job satisfaction
  - ➤ Excessive self expectation
  - ➤ Lack of PE fit

- **Toward Optional Stress Levels**
  - ➤ Working at larger institutions
  - ➤ Job satisfaction
  - ➤ Adequate funding
  - ➤ Being older
  - ➤ PE fit

The desirability of having a good fit between universities and their deans has never been more apparent. Public scrutiny of university efforts to educate large and diverse segments of society has brought with it a growing mistrust of the manner in which universities use their fiscal resources. These public demands for quality education at the right price call into question both administrative and instructional quality. Because deans form a critical link between university administration and classroom instruction, their ability to function well is a deciding factor in determining institutional effectiveness. Quite often, carrying out the directives of a provost run counter to protecting academic autonomy and faculty independence. Herein lies the challenge. To engage in educating students at optimal levels, the institution and its leadership must complement each other. There must be a good fit between deans and their colleges.

CHAPTER 6

Organizational Commitment and Intention to Leave: Why Deans Stay

Highly satisfied deans often experience lower levels of work-related stress. Lower levels of stress typically suggest that a dean and his or her organization are well matched. Such a statement, however, begs the question: Do deans exhibit organizational commitment or are they intent on leaving their current positions? And what factors might influence such a decision? Making the distinction is not necessarily a clear-cut exercise. Although organizational commitment and intention to leave seem to be dichotomous constructs, they are not. Deans who stay at one university for a long time may or may not be committed to the university. It is possible that they continue on where they are because they see no alternative, or they may be intent on leaving, but the opportunity to do so has not presented itself (March & Simon, 1958). In other words, for a dean to remain at a particular institution in a particular position does not guarantee that he or she is committed to the college or the university. By the same token, just because a dean intends to leave does not mean that he or she will actually do so. For universities, understanding why deans stay or think about leaving provides a first step toward ensuring that they maintain committed cadres of institutional leaders over time.

THE DIFFERENCE BETWEEN ORGANIZATIONAL COMMITMENT AND INTENTION TO LEAVE

Organizational commitment refers to the relative strength of a dean's identification with and involvement in a particular university. It manifests itself in a strong belief in and acceptance of an organization's goals and values, a willingness to exert considerable effort on behalf of the organization, and a strong desire to maintain membership in it. Organizational commitment goes beyond mere passive loyalty (Mowday, Porter, & Steers, 1982; Porter, Steers, Mowday, & Boulian, 1974). Current research suggests that organizational commitment has three components: affective, continuance, and normative commitment. *Affective commitment* reveals itself in a desire to stay involved because the organization is deemed supportive. *Continuance commitment* refers to a need to remain within a particular organization because the costs to change organizations are financially too high or no viable alternatives exist. Individuals who feel obligated to stay at an organization, perhaps because the organization has invested in training them, display *normative commitment*. In other words, deans remain at universities because they want, need, or feel obligated to do so. The strongest, and most desirable, type of organizational commitment is affective in nature (Clugston, 2000; Meyer & Allen, 1991, 1997). It follows that, from a university's perspective, much of why a dean stays at a university should be explained by a strong sense of loyalty or affective commitment; put simply, they want to stay.

Intention to leave is just that, a dean plans to sever his or her ties with the current employer and take up employment at another institution. It, along with actual turnover, is a well-established consequence of low organizational commitment (Abraham, 1999; Allen & Meyer, 1996; Becker, 1992; Clugston, 2000; Mathieu & Zajac, 1990; Tett & Meyer, 1993). Unlike other possible consequences—such as tardiness and absenteeism, in which the relationship with organizational commitment is modest, or job performance, in which the correlation is weak, at best—the strongest predictable behavioral outcome of organizational commitment is reduced turnover (Allen & Meyer, 1996; Becker, Billings, Eveleth, & Gilbert, 1996; Shore & Tetrick, 1991).

POSSIBLE INFLUENCES ON ORGANIZATIONAL COMMITMENT AND INTENTION TO LEAVE

Like intention to leave, other often tested phenomena (e.g., occupational commitment, job involvement, job satisfaction, and work ethic) are related yet clearly distinct from organizational commitment (Clugston, 2000; Eby, Freeman, Rush, & Lance, 1999; Meyer & Allen, 1991, 1997; Shore & Tetrick, 1991). One construct in particular, job satisfaction, bears mentioning. Nash (1994) found a strong correlation between job satisfaction and organizational commitment. Job satisfaction itself is multifaceted and depends, at least in part, on the nature of the work, details of remuneration, nature of promotional opportunities, characteristics of supervisors, and characteristics of co-workers (Smith, Kendall, & Hulin, 1969). It is perceived as an antecedent to both organizational commitment and intention to leave, as well as to actual turnover (Abraham, 1999; Atchinson & Lefferts, 1972; Herzberg, 1966; Mathieu & Hamel, 1989; Porter & Steers, 1973; Vroom, 1964; Welsch & LaVan, 1981). In addition, recent research suggests that the relationship between job satisfaction and organizational commitment is reciprocal, with organizational commitment also affecting job satisfaction (Kacmar et al., 1999; Vandenberg & Lance, 1992). Some researchers suggest that the relationship between organizational commitment and job satisfaction could be cyclical over a career and develop over time (Balfour & Wechsler, 1990; Reichers, 1986).

Other commonly cited antecedents to organizational commitment include age, tenure in a position, gender, organizational size, span of control, achievement motivation, sense of competence, stress, role conflict, and role ambiguity. The links, however, between personal characteristics (age, gender, and experience) and organizational commitment have proven weak and inconsistent over time (Meyer & Allen, 1997; Mowday et al., 1982). Even less evidence supports any relationship between structural features, such as organizational size and control issues, and commitment (Mowday et al., 1982). More consistency has been found concerning the influence of achievement motivation, perceived competence, stress, conflict, and ambiguity on organizational commitment (Balfour & Wechsler, 1990; Cook & Wall, 1980; Eby et al., 1999; Green, Anderson, & Shivers, 1996; Meyer & Allen, 1997; Mowday, Steers, & Porter, 1979).

THE MEANING OF DEAN ORGANIZATIONAL COMMITMENT, INTENTION TO LEAVE, AND OTHER SIGNIFICANT CONSTRUCTS

In this study, we defined organizational commitment in terms of loyalty. It is reflected in the statement "I hold strong loyalties to this university," to which deans indicated their degree of agreement on an ascending scale of 1 to 5. Intention to leave was captured in the statement "I will probably leave this university in two or three years." The statement "I could be as effective at another university as I am here" served as a surrogate for perceived competency. Both intention to leave and perceived competency were rated on the same scale as organizational commitment.

Job satisfaction in the study is a unidimensional construct composed of six variables: clarity of role, pace of work, workload, control of work environment, compensation package, and satisfaction with level of personal scholarship. Deans also rated a separate variable, overall job satisfaction. This particular variable captured more of the variance in job satisfaction across deans than did the composite variable, suggesting that there is more to dean job satisfaction than meets the eye. As a consequence, we used overall job satisfaction in the following analysis. We also conjectured that the perceived academic quality of the institution and its perceived environmental quality could be important determinants in a dean's commitment or intention to leave. For our purposes, academic quality is a combination of intellectual climate, institutional peer standing, quality of faculty, quality of instruction, academic ability of students, and collegiality among staff and faculty. Three variables—racial climate, gender equity, and quality of location—constitute environmental quality. Table 6.1 provides a complete listing of the variables that identify these constructs.

Deans in the study also rated a series of motivators of why they became administrators (deans). In addition, they indicated future career aspirations. We believe that their initial motivation for seeking the deanship

Table 6.1
Job Satisfaction and Institution Quality Constructs

Job Satisfaction
Clarity of Role
Pace of Work
Work Load
Control of Work Environment
Compensation Package
Satisfaction with Personal Scholarship Level
Institution's Academic Quality
Intellectual Climate
Institution's Peer Standing
Quality of Faculty
Quality of Instruction
Academic Ability of Students
Collegiality among Staff and Faculty
Institution's Environmental Quality
Racial Climate
Gender Equity
Quality of Location

combined with their career plans provides some perspective on overall motivation and desire for achievement. Table 6.2 highlights the choices to which deans responded. Most deans took their positions to contribute to and improve the college; but as we see later, what impacts their commitment levels has little to do with this sense of working toward the greater good of the university.

Finally, almost 20 percent of the deans in the study were sixty years or older, and most of them planned to retire shortly. Of the remaining deans, about 30 percent planned to return to faculty, 20 percent planned to seek another deanship or a nonacademic leadership position, and almost 30 percent will seek a higher academic leadership position. Less than 20 percent of current deans wanted no change at all. Table 6.2 lists the career options provided to deans in the study.

Once we had identified the constructs that we wanted to investigate, we examined them to determine whether any relationships existed between dean organizational commitment and job satisfaction, institutional academic quality, environmental quality, perceived competence, dean stress, role conflict, role ambiguity, and career motivation and aspirations. In addition, we took into account age, experience, gender, marital status, minority status, whether deans believed their institutions were good places to work, and whether they were promoted from within—all variables that have proven somewhat inconsistent in their relationships to organizational commitment but are nevertheless present in some populations. We also considered the same variables as they relate to a dean's intention to

Table 6.2
Career Motivators and Aspirations

I first became an administrator *because I wanted to* (for):
Contribute to and Improve the College
Financial Gain
Advancement of My Administrative Career
Power and Authority of the Position
Personal Growth
Influence the Development of Faculty
My next career move, given the opportunity, will be to:
Return to Faculty
Seek a Dean's Position at a Similar Institution
Seek a Dean's Position at a More Prestigious Institution
Seek a Higher Academic Leadership Position (e.g., Provost)
Change to a Non-academic Leadership Position
Stay Where I Am
Retire

leave. Finally, we examined organizational commitment as it relates to a dean's intention to leave, and vice versa.

DEANS AND ORGANIZATIONAL COMMITMENT

For deans in this study, organizational commitment seemed to increase with age, the number of years in the position, and the level of overall job satisfaction. Deans who were inside hires also seemed more committed to their universities than did those who were brought in from outside. If deans believed that they worked for universities that exhibited high academic quality, possessed good environmental quality (racial and gender climates and location), and, in general, were good places to work, they tended to be more committed to the organizations. Finally, higher levels of work-related stress (within reason) seemed to enhance organizational commitment, suggesting that optimal stress levels may energize deans in their work environments.

In contrast, even though role conflict did not influence organizational commitment, role ambiguity did. Those deans who experienced greater ambiguity were less committed to their universities. If deans took their positions for financial gain, they were less committed. If they intended to leave and take a deanship at a more prestigious university, there were less committed. If they believed that they lacked competence to do the job and to be effective at another university, they tended to exhibit less organizational commitment. Finally, race, gender, and marital status did not seem to impact the level of organizational commitment in deans in this study (see Table 6.3).

DEANS AND INTENTION TO LEAVE

As might be expected, deans who were less satisfied in their current positions and less committed to their universities exhibited a greater intent to leave. If, however, they believed that their universities were good places to work and they were committed to their universities, they demonstrated less of an intent to leave. Being an inside hire also seemed to lessen a dean's desire to leave. The intention to leave increased with age. Deans who had taken their position to advance their administrative careers were more inclined to leave; but if they sought power and authority or planned to move to higher administrative positions, deans tended not to leave.

In contrast, if deans wanted to remain deans but wanted to do so at more prestigious institutions, they obviously intended to leave their current employers. If deans planned to move out of administration and back into the faculty ranks, they were less apt to plan on leaving. If they were content in what they were doing, they also exhibited little desire to leave. If they be-

Table 6.3
Influences on Organizational Commitment in Deans

Increases	Decreases
Age	Took the Position for Financial Gain
Experience	Would Like a Deanship at a More
Inside Hire	Prestigious University
Overall Job Satisfaction	Perceived Competence
University Is a Good Place to Work	Intention to Leave
Dean Stress	Role Ambiguity
Academic Quality of the University	
Environmental Quality of the University	

lieved that they were competent and could be effective elsewhere, they were more likely to think about leaving. In addition, the level of role conflict they experienced seemed to influence the decision; the greater the conflict, the stronger the intent to leave. Finally, gender, marital status, experience, and academic and environmental quality did not seem to impact the intention of deans to leave, but racial status did. White deans were less likely to be intent on leaving; deans of color were more apt to plan on moving to another institution (see Table 6.4).

WHY DEANS STAY

Consistent with previous research findings, the gender and marital status of deans in this study did not influence either organizational commitment or intention to leave. Similarly, racial standing did not bear on organizational commitment, but it did impact deans' intentions to leave. One has to wonder whether deans of color perceive that they have more options available to them, especially in terms of administrative career advancement in the current job market, than do white deans. Interestingly, age positively impacted both organizational commitment and intention to leave, suggesting that if deans plan to stay at one institution, their organizational commitment grows over time; if they plan to leave, the urge to do so grows stronger as they grow older.

Several variables had inverse effects on the two overarching constructs, and the end results seem to make sense. For example, deans who were inside hires tended to be more committed and less apt to leave than were deans who were brought into an organization from outside. The reverse was true of perceived competency. If deans believed that they could be effective elsewhere, they were more intent on leaving. In other words, deans who believed that they could do the same or a better job at another university exhibited lower levels of organizational commitment. This, perhaps, implies

Table 6.4
Influences on Intention to Leave in Deans

Increases	Decreases
Age	Inside Hire
Would Like a Deanship at a More Prestigious	Took the Position for Power
University	Overall Job Satisfaction
Role Conflict	Plan to Return to Faculty or Seek a Higher
Perceived Competence	Academic Administrative Position
Minority Status	Have no Interest in Changing
	University Is a Good Place to Work
	Organizational Commitment
	Being White

that if they stay at their current universities, they do so not out of a sense of loyalty but because the costs of leaving are too high, or they see no viable alternatives (in Meyer and Allen's terms, continuance commitment). The other variables that influenced both organizational commitment and intention to leave, but in opposite directions, also make sense. If deans were satisfied in their jobs, believed they work at good institutions, and had no intention of leaving, they tended to exhibit higher levels of organizational commitment. Likewise, if they were dissatisfied at work, did not like where they worked, and were not particularly committed to the organization, they were more apt to leave.

Five work-related variables—stress, conflict, ambiguity, job satisfaction, and institutional quality (academic and environmental)—are particularly worth noting. Although the influence of each of these variables is partly captured in one or more of the other constructs (i.e., conflict and ambiguity influence the level of job satisfaction deans experience), they also directly impact either organizational commitment or intention to leave. The positive influence of work-related stress on organizational commitment seems to suggest that some level of job stress is desirable, possibly because it helps to challenge deans to do their best.

The negative relationships between organizational commitment and ambiguity and intention to leave and conflict are more troublesome. In the first instance, this finding seems to indicate that when deans do not have a clear sense of where university priorities lie and do not know what is expected of them, organizational commitment suffers. As a result, they may plan to leave; if they stay on, they may do so out of necessity rather than a sense of commitment. In the second instance, if too many of the demands placed on deans are at odds with each other or force deans to act in ways counter to their own fundamental values, deans will leave. Somewhat surprising was the finding that academic and environmental quality issues impacted only degree of commitment, not intention to leave.

Finally, some interesting dynamics fall out when we examine motivation and career aspiration variables. For example, none of the intrinsic motivators, such as a desire to contribute, personal growth, or the development of faculty, seem to influence either commitment or intention to leave. The motivation variables that do carry weight in the decision to leave or in the level of commitment are achievement driven (financial gain, career advancement, power and authority) and externally measurable. Taking the deanship for financial gain negatively impacts commitment, suggesting that perhaps some deans believe that they are not paid enough for the work they do. A dean's motivation to advance his or her career seems to add to any impetus to leave, but not necessarily if he or she has a desire for power and authority. In this instance, deans may believe that they have more power at their present universities than they would if they moved to other institutions. There also seems to be some connection between the type of position a dean sees as his or her next career move and commitment and intention to leave. In the first case, if deans want to remain deans but at more prestigious institutions, they are less apt to be committed to their current places of employment and more apt to be intent on leaving. Other future career options did not appear to affect organizational commitment, but they did influence intention to leave. If deans wanted to remain in their current positions, they had no intention of leaving. If they planned on returning to faculty status, they were less inclined to think about leaving, suggesting that an unofficial (or in some cases, probably, an official) "golden parachute" exists for deans at their current universities. Interestingly, deans who will seek higher academic administrative positions, such as provost, appeared to believe that they stand a better chance of securing such a position at their current institutions than at other universities. They may hold this opinion because of groundwork already laid through internal networking and politicking. As such, they demonstrate less of a tendency to express the intention to leave.

IMPLICATIONS

The good news is that almost 50 percent of the deans in the study felt extremely strong loyalties to their current universities, and less than 20 percent were very intent on leaving. The bad news is that roughly 30 percent of them said that they were somewhat loyal to or ambivalent about their universities. These deans stay because the costs of leaving are too high or they see no viable alternatives. This type of commitment, based on continuance rather than loyalty, results in actions on the part of deans that are self-serving but not necessarily beneficial to the university.

If a university is not perceived as a particularly great place to work because institutional quality is lacking, or it has ill-defined institutional goals, or deans face conflicting demands, it should take notice. These are deep-seeded, systemic difficulties that deans alone cannot remedy. Universities that perceive that they have problems often bring deans in from outside to "raise the bar," to whip the college into shape, so to speak. However, such moves may not always provide the best answer. Deans who are raised up within the system appear to be more committed to their universities than deans brought in from the outside. In reality, inside candidates should not be automatically discounted as somehow less qualified. If they have demonstrated leadership ability and understand what the university and college need to move forward, they may be able to build support and trust among faculty much more easily than an outsider can. The logical conclusion here is that perhaps the first place to look for good deans is at home. By the same token, if good deans believe they are undersupported, undervalued, and unappreciated, they may choose to look elsewhere. If they remain, such deans often devolve into mere placeholding administrators, biding their time until retirement.

CHAPTER 7

Female and Minority Deans and the Keys to Success

Few deans take leadership positions because they want to fail. To the contrary, they want to succeed and believe they can. In essence, most deans hope and expect to leave their colleges better off than when they found them (Kouzes & Posner, 1993). The first step—securing the position—remains a difficult task for women and minorities, however.

The *glass ceiling* is the euphemism used to explain this phenomenon. Women and persons of color can see the top rung of the ladder, so to speak, but they can't quite reach it (U.S. Department of Labor, 1991). The ceiling metaphorically represents the cumulative effect of both visible and invisible barriers to entry and career progression. Prejudice, discrimination, and stereotyping—all contribute. We make decisions based on preconceived notions of leadership as a male construct; we discriminate based on ease and comfort (we simply prefer people who look and think like us). We continue to hold gender-based behavioral expectations and adhere to racial profiles that color our estimates of professional potential of others. For instance, traditional values that hold women responsible for household duties and child rearing sometimes conflict with the career aspirations of contemporary women. To complicate matters further, colleges and universities have difficulty identifying white women and people of color with high leadership potential; once they do, new deans from underrepresented groups often experience a sense of isolation, in part, because few have role models and mentors (Bell and Nkomo, 1998; Braddock & McPartland,

1987; Gherardi, 1995; Hughs, 1988; Jamieson, 1995; Moore & Amey, 1988; Morrison, 1996; Oakes, 1999; Pettigrew & Martin, 1987; Shakeshaft, 1985; Williams & Best, 1990).

This last finding, in particular, is troublesome. Consistently, women suggest that the greatest benefit for them at the beginning of their administrative careers is having professional role models (Twale & Jelenik, 1996). In addition, mentors seem instrumental in securing administrative positions for women more often than they do for men (Hill & Ragland, 1995; Hubbard & Robinson, 1998). Mentoring and networking are also crucial for men of color, particularly African Americans (Astin & Leland, 1991; Hersi, 1993; Morrison, 1996; Thomas, 1990, 1993).

In reality, racism and sexism are part and parcel of the American identity and, although universities are populated by individuals who believe they work in communities of diversity, we are little better off than the rest of society. In fact, we simply mirror it (Banks, 1995; Bennett, 1995; Franklin, 1993; West, 1993). Women remain a minority because they lack access to power. That is not to say that women do not become deans, but their presence remains concentrated in feminized disciplines, such as nursing and, to a lesser extent, education. Minority males also tend to be clustered in fields, such as education. Overall, white women have fared better than women and men of color (Butler & Walter, 1991; Hubbard & Robinson, 1998; Konrad & Pfeffer, 1991; Tedrow & Rhoads, 1999; Warner & DeFleur, 1993).

DEANS IN THE STUDY

The following demographic sketch (Table 7.1) helps to illustrate this point. Of the deans in this study, 41 percent were women; almost half of these were deans of nursing colleges, and a quarter worked in education colleges. Another 23 percent headed liberal arts colleges. Only 4 percent were deans of business colleges. In contrast, men were more typically found in business (27 percent), liberal arts (33 percent), and education (32 percent), with fewer men in colleges of nursing (7 percent). A typical gender distribution pattern in the deanship across all disciplines (not just the four in this study) would find less than 25 percent of the deanships filled by women, with virtually no female deans in some disciplines.

The minority population in this study stood at 12 percent, one-half of whom were African American. This figure may be slightly high, again because of the colleges (education, business, nursing, and liberal arts) surveyed. Most deans of color were in either education (35 percent) or liberal arts (31 percent). Smaller percentages of these deans were in nursing (20 percent) and business (13 percent).

The length of time in the current position (Table 7.2) varied by college and across race and gender, with women and minorities holding their positions for shorter amounts of time in most instances. The greatest discrepancies can be seen in business, with male deans holding the position, on average, more than one year longer than female deans, and minority deans holding the position for less than three years. Even in the field of nursing, a discipline dominated by women, male deans served more than one year longer than did their female counterparts. Deans of color in nursing colleges, as a group, served longer than either men or women as a group.

Less than two-thirds of all deans experienced mentoring relationships (Table 7.3). Men were far less likely than women to be mentored. Most men were mentored by white men. Women, in general, were less likely to be mentored by men. Male minority deans were more likely than white male deans to be mentored by women. Female deans of color were more apt to be mentored than were male deans of color but less likely to be engaged in this type of relationship than were white female deans; they were also much less likely to have white mentors than any other group. More than half of those mentored were sponsored from within their own institutions; minority males were mentored by individuals outside their institutions more often than white male deans or female deans, however. These last

Table 7.1
Distribution of Deans across Disciplines

	Business	Liberal Arts	Education	Nursing
Men	27%	33%	32%	7%
Women	4%	23%	25%	47%
Minority	13%	31%	35%	20%

Table 7.2
Years in Current Position

College	Male	Female	Minority
Business	5.2 years	3.7 years	2.8 years
Liberal Arts	5.6 years	4.6 years	5.8 years
Education	6.2 years	4.4 years	3.9 years
Nursing	7.6 years	6.3 years	7.8 years

findings suggest that although support systems may be important for some deans, other deans seem to succeed of their own volition.

THE KEYS TO LEADERSHIP SUCCESS

Even though access may be limited and mentors and role models few, women and minorities do succeed in leadership roles, and in the deanship in particular (Astin & Leland, 1991; Jamieson, 1995; Thomas & Gabarro, 1999). What is it about persisters that allows them to succeed in top-level executive positions? Thomas and Gabarro (1999) studied executives and managers—mostly white males, a few females, a small number of persons of color (mostly African American)—in three large corporations that have historically furthered the careers of individuals from underrepresented groups. They compared minority and white leaders in order to delineate the factors between groups that helped to explain why executives of color in the study succeeded. They suggest that successful minority leaders possess three personal resources: confidence, competence, and credibility. Although these assets are important to all leaders, regardless of race, ethnicity, or gender, they appear to be extremely important for women and minorities. Based on a firm conviction that deans are more similar to, than different from, their counterparts in corporate America, we suggest that deans, and particularly white women and people of color, must also have these three resources (Astin & Leland, 1991; Bennett & Shayner, 1988; Moore, 1990).

Confidence, competence, and credibility overlap and intertwine. The terms themselves are sometimes used interchangeably. Quite often one concept is subordinated to another. For instance, Thomas and Gabarro (1999) assert that self-confidence may be a person's most important resource. Kouzes and Posner (1993, 1995) believe that credibility is most

Table 7.3
Mentoring Support as Leaders

	Mentored	Mentor at Same Institution	Male Mentor	White Mentor
Male Deans	50%	64%	85%	92%
Female Deans	63%	65%	49%	89%
Minority Deans	52%	52%	64%	50%
Minority Female Deans	56%	59%	48%	41%

critical, and Jamieson (1995) speaks only of competence. Many writers, however, either explicitly or implicitly, refer to these three constructs as crucial components of leadership (Hesselbein, Goldsmith, & Beckhard, 1996; Kanter, 1977; Koestenbaum, 1991).

Confidence

Leadership has everything to do with what we think of ourselves. Self-confidence is a belief in a dean's past achievements, current competence, and future ability to succeed (Thomas & Gabarro, 1999). As leaders, deans must believe that they can get things done and that they can make a difference (Bandura, 1986; Kouzes & Posner, 1993). Self-confidence provides a sense of internal security that bolsters a dean's ability to ward off doubts, to withstand attacks on his or her credibility, and to maintain a self-concept that is relatively immune to the self-fulfilling effects of stereotypes (Thomas & Gabarro, 1999). Minorities and women, in particular, may be vulnerable to stereotyping of inferiority, which undermines confidence (Shakeshaft, 1985, Steele and Aronson, 1995). Self-confidence is sharply distinguished from arrogance and egotism, which often point to insecurity and sometimes mask incompetence (Hesselbein et al., 1996). It enables leaders to undertake difficult ventures necessary to meet goals. It makes them willing, prudent risk-takers and allows them to have confidence in and support the advancement of other people in the organization (Hesselbein et al., 1996). It is essential to promoting and sustaining consistent efforts. Each success builds up a sense of competence and confidence (Kouzes and Posner, 1993). Central to gaining confidence in the workplace is the quality of a dean's work relations with supervisors and peers. Minority deans typically need extremely high levels of confidence to rise to the executive level (Thomas and Gabarro, 1999).

Competence

Competence refers to a dean's ability to add value to an organization because of the technical knowledge base that he or she possesses. A fundamental grounding in one or more areas of expertise in the organization, coupled with the capacity to learn from experience, allows leaders to intuitively sense how disparate elements of a college are connected, and in turn produce new insights about organizational well-being (Thomas & Gabarro, 1999). In addition to technical competence, deans must demonstrate well-honed leadership skills. The combination of technical competence and leadership skills provides them with the ability to challenge, inspire, enable, model, and encourage members of their colleges (Kouzes & Posner, 1993). Competence starts with high self-imposed performance expectations and a strong work ethic (Hill & Ragland, 1995). It matures through constructive use of ongoing feedback and a continued mastery of new and broader skills (Kouzes & Posner, 1995; Thomas & Gabarro, 1999). To do this requires an understanding of one's motivation and a desire for sustained learning. Thomas and Gabarro contend that white executives typically gain competence through promotions that expose them to new operational areas and challenges. In contrast, executives of color gain competency through depth of mastery rather than breadth of experience. Such depth compensates for being left out of white peer networks. In the end, reality suggests that minority executives and women, in particular, are held to a different standard—one that demands that they work harder and do better. In other words, they must be highly competent (Hill & Ragland, 1995; Jamieson, 1995; Thomas & Gabarro, 1999).

Credibility

Credibility is the most elusive of the three personal resources. It depends on personal expectations for successful performance, integrity, and a dean's impact on core college efforts (Thomas & Gabarro, 1999). In essence, credibility is a combination of being honest, reliable, forward thinking, inspiring, and competent (Hesselbein et al., 1996; Kouzes & Posner, 1993, 1995). To such a litany, Kanter (1977) added power. Power arises from access to social networks and important work assignments (Kanter, 1977; Thomas & Gabarro, 1999). To this end, relations with faculty, other deans, students, future employers, alumni, provosts, and presidents, combined with demonstrated performance, directly influence credibility (Hesselbein et al., 1996; Thomas & Gabarro, 1999). People invest in the careers of others because they view them as credible. Leaders who share power through collaboration are, significantly, more likely to be seen as credible. For some, credibility with a sense of direction provides a telling definition of leadership (Kouzes & Posner, 1993).

DEANS AND CONFIDENCE, COMPETENCE, AND CREDIBILITY

To examine deans' perceptions of competence, confidence, and credibility as they pertain to perceived success in the deanship, we built one relational regression model and tested it across four subpopulations of the data set. In each case, we used the same four variables. Perception of success (the independent variable) was captured in the statement "I am an effective leader" (rated in ascending from 1 to 5). Perceived confidence was measured by responses to the statement "I am confident in my leadership abilities"; competency in the statement "I could be as effective elsewhere." Credibility was reflected in the responses to a composite variable consisting of four statements about leadership behavior: "I can be relied on," "I follow through on commitments," "I keep promises," and "I am consistent in word and actions" (alpha = .75; all rated on the same 5–point scale). The subpopulations we examined included white males, white females, minority females, and minority males.

Perceived Leadership Success

As a precursor to testing the model, we examined each of the variables separately to identify any significant perceptual differences across subgroups (Table 7.4). In general, females rated their leadership success higher than did their male counterparts. There was no discernible difference between white male and female deans, but minority female deans rated themselves higher than minority male deans did. No difference existed between the two male subgroups; however, minority females rated themselves as more successful than white female deans rated themselves. Half of the minority female deans rated this variable 5; no one in this group awarded herself a 1 or 2. In the other three groups, less than 30 percent rated themselves so high. A few white male deans suggested very low levels of success (1 or 2); the lowest rating minority males used was 3. (See Table 7.4.)

Confidence

Slightly over one-third of both male (38 percent) and female deans (37 percent) in the study assigned the highest rating, 5, in confidence to themselves (Table 7.5). No significant differences appeared among white males, white females, and minority males, but minority female deans were more likely to rate themselves confident than were members of the other subgroups.

Table 7.4
Differences in Perceptions of Leadership Success

	Mean	% Rated 5
White Males	4.1	25%
White Females	4.2	29%
Minority Males	4.1	26%
Minority Females	4.5	50%

Table 7.5
Difference in Perceptions of Confidence

	Mean	% Rated 5
White Males	4.2	38%
White Females	4.1	32%
Minority Males	4.2	40%
Minority Females	4.6	65%

Competence

Overall, 42 percent of the males in the study rated competence 5, and 45 percent of female deans did so. No significant differences in perceptions of competence existed between men and women in the study. Significant differences did exist between white and minority deans, in general, and white and minority females, specifically with minority female deans assigning a higher value to this variable (Table 7.6).

Credibility

Women, as a whole, believed they possessed higher levels of credibility than did men (mean score for women was 4.54 and for men was 4.48). However, only about one-quarter of either men or women in the study thought of themselves as highly credible leaders (rating 5). Again, minority female deans rated this variable significantly more characteristic of themselves than did other groups (Table 7.7).

By Thomas and Gabarro's standards, all three personal resources—confidence, competence, and credibility—should, at least for minority deans, be significant contributors to leadership success. However, when we look at each of the four subgroups, some interesting patterns emerge. For both white males and females, all three constructs are significantly important. For each of the minority subsets, however, this relationship does not hold. For minority female deans, only self-confidence bears a significant relationship to leadership success. In some respects, this finding verifies Thomas and Gabarro's assertion that self-confidence is the most important resource for minority executives. For minority males, competency and confidence were significantly related to success, suggesting perhaps a realization that self-confidence can carry a dean only so far. Interestingly, credibility was not a significant factor for either minority men or minority women in the study (Table 7.8).

Table 7.6
Difference in Perceptions of Competence

	Mean	% Rated 5
White Males	4.1	40%
White Females	4.2	42%
Minority Males	4.4	51%
Minority Females	4.5	64%

Table 7.7
Difference in Perceptions of Credibility

	Mean	% Rated 5
White Males	4.5	26%
White Females	4.5	26%
Minority Males	4.5	26%
Minority Females	4.6	30%

IMPLICATIONS

This data set does not allow us to look at generational differences across deans, but the results reported in this chapter suggest that some may exist. For instance, if we operate from the premise that confidence, competence, and credibility are all important to leadership success, it appears that white male and female deans have arrived. Minority male deans may be on their way, in that they recognize that confidence may not be enough and they need to be competent as well. And minority female deans are still relying on self-confidence to carry the day.

If we look at employment trends over the past forty years, white males have definitely been in leadership positions the longest, followed by white females, then minority males (especially African-American males), and, finally, minority females. Such a pattern seems to be hinted at by the average length of time in the current position in the most male-dominated college in the study, business. Whereas white male deans in the study have been in the position an average of 5.2 years, we see a continually shortened tenure as we examine each successive group. White females have served for 4 years, minority males for 2.9 years, and minority females for 2.5 years. If this is, indeed, the pattern for moving underrepresented populations into the deanship, fully realizing the importance of all three resources may, in

Table 7.8
Leadership Success Models by Population

White Males	Successful Leadership = Confidence + Competence + Credibility
White Females	Successful Leadership = Confidence + Competence + Credibility
Minority Males	Successful Leadership = Confidence + Competence
Minority Females	Successful Leadership = Confidence

Note: Each equation shows those personal resources that were statistically significant to the subgroup.

essence, be a matter of generational maturation—with credibility, the least quantifiable and most intangible asset, being the last resource to be developed or at least fully recognized by deans.

The mentoring experiences of female deans do suggest a growing awareness of the importance of this kind of support for underrepresented groups. Yet deans of color, including women, were the group least mentored. Such a finding points to a mentoring pecking order of sorts, which more than likely stalls deans of color within existing leadership succession patterns. A confounding issue may lie in the source of mentoring for deans of color. White deans tend to be mentored by others at their own institutions. Deans of color seem to depend on institutional outsiders for this type of support. Such arrangements may actually disadvantage some deans of color because no matter how well intentioned their mentors may be, they simply do not know the political ins and outs of the institutions where their mentees currently work. In the end, this situation may dampen the prospects of maturing into effective leaders for deans of color. At best, it most certainly could slow their progress.

CHAPTER 8

Balance, Trade-offs, and Life after the Deanship

At the beginning of this book, we presented a brief sketch of Dean Morgan's day. It points to someone caught up in the immediacy of management, fully ensconced in the role of college administrator, with little time to take on leadership, let alone pursue personal endeavors. Subsequent chapters suggest that the Dean Morgans of the world do indeed struggle for balance. In business, the primary balance issue hinges on the proportion of time that executives are expected to devote to work-related responsibilities in relation to time allocated to family, friends, and personal activities. A second balance issue that impacts the effectiveness of CEOs revolves around the relative emphasis they place on leadership (dealing with issues of organizational purpose) and management (dealing with on-going operational issues that determine organizational solvency and success) (Bass, 1990, 1998; Friedman, Christensen, & DeGroot, 1998; Gmelch et al., 1999; Lindberg, 1995). We suggest that academic deans grapple with an additional balancing act: aligning leadership and management responsibilities with scholarship. Furthermore, we suggest that the balances they strike help to determine their effectiveness as deans.

Universities charge deans with enhancing and sustaining the quality and reputation of their colleges. This is a collective task, which can be both stressful and complex. Effectively engaging in it requires that deans seek agreement about priorities and cooperation and trust among college constituencies and that they coordinate efforts and define and maintain boundaries (Yukl, 1998). For the most part, deans who participated in the study believed they were effective leaders (Table 8.1). Only four deans rated themselves less than 3 (on a 5-point ascending scale) when asked if they were effective leaders. Fifteen percent rated themselves 3 or below (moderately effective), 57 percent rated themselves 4 (effective), and the remaining 28 percent awarded themselves the highest rating (5, highly effective). Women and minority deans typically regarded themselves as more effective than white male deans thought themselves to be. Twenty-six percent of male deans perceived themselves to be highly effective; 38 percent of the minorities and 32 percent of female deans saw themselves in the same light. Of those who believed they were only moderately effective or ineffective, 17 percent were male, 12 percent were minority, and 13 percent were female. If we consider the fact that less than 60 percent of the participants in the study were male, a disproportionate percentage of those who rated themselves only moderately effective (≤ 3) were male (66 percent).

To gain a better understanding of how deans in the study dealt with balancing issues, we examined two pairs of these relationships: management duties against leadership responsibilities and the pursuit of scholarship against the seductiveness of administrative authority (leadership and management). To do so, we compared deans who perceived themselves as highly effective (5) with those who believed they were moderately effective (3) at best. We believe that arriving at the proper combination of each polarity impacts a dean's ability to balance professional career and personal life.

Table 8.1
Self-Perceptions of Leadership Effectiveness

Rating	Female Deans	Male Deans	Minority Deans
Not Effective	.00	.00[1]	.00
Slightly Effective	.00[2]	.00[3]	.00
Moderately Effective	.13	.17*	.12
Effective	.55*	.47	.50
Very Effective	.32*	.26	.38*

Note: A 5-point rating scale (5 = very effective) was used.
*Indicates significant differences from all other deans
1. One white male dean rated himself not effective.
2. One female dean rated herself slightly effective.
3. Two white male deans rated themselves slightly effective.

BALANCING MANAGEMENT AND LEADERSHIP

The management-leadership dilemma that deans face is quite simple. The daily to-dos of running a college, such as recordkeeping, filing reports, and dealing with personnel squabbles, wage war against "what we're all about." Deans are held to standards of compliance and conformity but constantly receive signals that encourage raising the research productivity of college faculty, increasing the quality of programs, and diversifying the faculty, students, and staff. All of these require creativity and innovation.

On the one hand, effective managers ensure that the daily operations of organizations run smoothly. They tend toward the use of control and command mechanisms; organize around goals, tasks, and agendas; focus attention on the issue at hand; communicate well; match resources with the requirements of the work to be completed; monitor progress; and understand what motivates people (Bensimon et al., 1989; Burns, 1978; Heifetz, 1994; Hollander, 1964; Jacobs, 1970). In short, managers concentrate power in order to accomplish the work at hand.

Leadership, on the other hand, has to do with creating a culture in which managers can be successful. Leadership involves a certain degree of flexibility and a willingness to share authority and responsibilities. Academic leaders, by our definition, pursue collective ideals by empowering their colleges to change their situations for the better (Astin & Astin, 2001; Matusak, 1997; Mintzberg, 1998). They have a passion for work, an empathy for others, and the social skills necessary to build rapport and find common ground. They strive to personally impact their followers by shifting responsibility to those with the greatest vested interests. They identify relevant challenges, focus people on crucial issues, and move them away from unnecessary distractions (Bennis & Nanus, 1985; Heifetz, 1994).

Recent literature suggests that truly successful leaders combine both leadership and management (Allen & Cherrey, 2000; Bass, 1998; Yukl, 1998). Leadership keeps a college pointed toward a vision or purpose. Management ensures that day-to-day operations of the college run efficiently. It provides the wherewithal to reach the vision. The connotation here is that deans must perform the day-to-day actions of operational management, but not at the expense of the generation of ideas and the formation of collective visions of the future. In so doing, effective deans make people feel significant and instill in them the notions that learning and competence matter, that people are the community, and that work is exciting (Bennis, 1999; Chliwniak, 1997; DePree, 1992; Helgesen, 1990, 1995; Regan & Brooks, 1995; Wheatley, 1992). Bass (1998) suggests that such a combination is indeed desirable, but that more emphasis should be placed on those responsibilities, that fall under the definition of leadership.

To determine whether deans in the study favored one strategy over the other or valued leadership and management equally, we constructed two 9-item task scales and compared groups of deans across scales (Table 8.2). The first scale includes dean responsibilities that approximate our trihedral definition of academic leadership: deans build community, set direction, and empower others. For deans in our study, leadership required that they carry out tasks, such as maintaining a conducive work climate, soliciting ideas from others to improve the college, and encouraging faculty, chairperson, and staff professional development. The second reflects our understanding of college management and includes operational tasks, such as fostering good teaching; recruiting, supervising, and evaluating faculty and chairpersons; and managing resources.

Highly effective deans seemed to tip the balance somewhat in favor of leadership tasks. Mean scores for each scale were management, 4.32, and leadership, 4.41. Although the difference in these mean scores seems slight, the scores are significantly different. In contrast, moderately effective deans rate leadership and management tasks equally important: management, 3.95; leadership, 3.97. When we compare highly effective deans (5) with moderately effective deans (≤3), highly effective deans rated both the management and leadership scales higher than did moderately effective deans. Female deans and deans of color consistently rated these scales higher than did white males.

Table 8.2
Management and Leadership Scales

Management	Leadership
Foster good teaching.	Maintain conducive work climate.
Recruit and select chairs and faculty.	Foster diversity.
Evaluate chair and faculty performance.	Plan and conduct leadership team meetings.
Assign duties to chairs and directors.	Solicit ideas to improve the college.
Supervise department chairs and directors.	Develop and initiate long-range college goals.
Manage college resources.	Communicate goals to constituents.
Financial planning and budgeting.	Encourage employee professional development.
Maintain effective communication across units.	Represent the college to the administration.
Maintain accurate college records.	Obtain and manage external funds.
reliability score: alpha = .69	reliability score: alpha = .75

Table 8.3
Management/Leadership Balance across Deans

	Highly Effective Deans	Moderately Effective Deans	Male Deans	Female Deans	Minority Deans
Management Scale	4.32*	3.95	4.11	4.22*	4.30*
Leadership Scale	4.41*	3.97	4.11	4.32*	4.43*

*Indicates significant differences from other deans

BALANCING SYNERGISTIC LEADERSHIP AND SCHOLARSHIP

In their everyday work lives, deans face a philosophical dilemma that demands that they place relative values on their roles as scholars and their responsibilities as leaders and managers. Universities often hire deans for their scholarly endeavors and research reputations. In fact, Cronin and Crawford (1999) suggest that deans must be well read and published in their area of expertise to be taken seriously by faculty. The message sent reflects an expectation of continued scholarly work, but the arena into which deans are thrust does not support the realization of such expectations. Deans rapidly move from a professional life built on long periods of contemplation and writing to calendars filled with fifteen-minute time slots and days crammed with meeting upon meeting, week after week (Sarros & Gmelch, 1996). In reality, they become casualties of someone else's agenda.

Conventional wisdom suggests that people change their behavior to match their beliefs. Therefore, if deans believe that their continued involvement in scholarly activities is important, they will make time for it. In reality, however, people adjust their belief systems to match current behaviors (Lindberg, 1995). They rationalize. Deans tell themselves, "Daily administrative tasks must be done, and I'm the one who has to do them." Guilt becomes a common bedfellow of scholar-deans. Although they have reprioritized their roles, weighing in in favor of administrative responsibilities, they have not done away with the stress associated with research activities. These deans seek to mitigate a tension between remaining true to their scholarship and performing properly as administrators (Grace, 1982; Mintzberg, 1998). The highest priority as a faculty member has become the least important task as dean, precisely because it is a time-consuming, long-term effort (Gmelch & Chan, 1994; Wolverton, Montez, & Gmelch, 2000).

To examine this balance issue, we computed two additional scales and compared their average scores across deans. The first scale, synergistic leadership, combines the leadership and management scales into one entity. Synergism refers to the conduct of two or more sets of activities to achieve an effect, which cannot be accomplished by employing either set of activities individually. Synergistic leadership, then, refers to the notion that effective deans must engage in both leadership and management. (Table 8.2 list all management and leadership tasks that combine to form synergistic leadership.) One without the other results in less than optimal dean and college performance. The second scale incorporates four dean tasks: remaining current in one's discipline, maintaining one's scholarship program and associated professional activities, maintaining and fostering personal professional growth, and demonstrating scholarship through regularly publishing and presenting papers (see Table 8.4).

All deans appear to have trouble balancing synergistic leadership with being a scholar (Table 8.5). The mean scores across all deans on synergistic leadership (4.2) and scholarship (3.5) suggest a reordering of priorities. The fact that deans are not particularly satisfied with their level of scholarly activity also implies that an imbalance exists. Nor does it seem to matter whether deans rate themselves as highly effective. Highly effective deans, on average, rated synergistic leadership 4.36 and scholarship 3.73. Those deans who believed they were only moderately effective rated syner-

Table 8.4
Scholarship Scale

Remain current with my own academic discipline.
Maintain my own scholarship program and associated professional activities.
Maintain and foster my own professional growth.
Demonstrate scholarship and model scholarship by publishing and/or presenting papers regularly.
reliability score: alpha = .84

Table 8.5
Synergistic Leadership/Scholarship Balance across Deans

	Highly Effective Deans	Moderately Effective Deans	Male Deans	Female Deans	Minority Deans
Synergistic Leadership	4.36*	3.95	4.11	4.76*	4.37*
Scholarship	3.73*	3.31	3.36	4.27*	3.92*

*Indicates significant differences from other deans

gistic leadership 3.95 and scholarship 3.31. (Highly effective deans do rate both these task categories as significantly more important than do less effective deans.) In retrospect, it seems that deans, for the most part, have built scholarly reputations. Now their livelihoods depend on administrative acumen. Such conflicting demands require that deans consciously evaluate and shift their priorities.

BALANCING PERSONAL LIFE WITH PROFESSIONAL CAREER

Cumulatively, the efforts to properly balance management with leadership and synergistic leadership with scholarship, and the degree to which deans are successful in doing so, contribute to or detract from their ability to balance their professional and personal lives. Achieving balance means making choices and enjoying those choices. The administrative arm of the academy functions under expectations biased by an unwritten code. Simply put, career advancement often goes to those who put in long hours at work and allocate additional time to university and college social activities. Being seen becomes the ultimate criterion for ascension in the ranks. This infringement on their privacy is a high stressor in their lives (Friedman et al., 1998; Wolverton, Montez, Gmelch, 2000). Under the press of institutional and self-imposed commitments, deans experience the erosion of leisure time and social relationships. Stressed-out deans typically work their personal lives right out of existence. Even on vacation they have to be busy to feel okay, checking in with the office, working on reports that can wait or be written by someone else. Time spent relaxing or just plain having fun is time ill-spent, in the eyes of guilt-ridden deans.

In establishing a work-life balance, time is the issue. Personal and professional priorities emanate from a vision of who the dean is personally, as a family member, and as a professional. It culminates in determining what it means to have an optimal experience as a dean. For example, deans who attempt to stay involved in research sometimes forget to set priorities that include research as part of their professional agenda. Under such a scenario, research and writing eat into whatever personal life they have because their boundaries are too permeable or simply do not exist. To gain balance within their professional lives, either time must be set aside for scholarly projects or a conscious choice to forego research efforts must be made.

Striking a work-life balance can lead to more satisfying personal lives and efficiency in work processes (Austin & Rice, 1998; Friedman et al., 1998). Clarity in professional and personal purpose, recognition and support of the whole-person concept (i.e., personal and professional), and experimenting with the way work is done are three methods for alleviating the conflict between work and personal priorities (Bailyn, Fletcher, & Kolb, 1997; Friedman et al., 1998). Effective deans realize that an enriching personal life makes for a more productive dean (Coughlan, 1994: Friedman et al., 1998; Grace, 1982; Hesselbein et. al., 1996).

The more contentious stressors for deans (especially women) include official commitments that must be attended to outside the regular workday and conflict with personal activities (Bailyn, 1989, 1993; McCracken, 2000; Posig, 1999; Smulyan, 2000). Social obligations expected of deans—such as joining clubs to promote college and university visibility, hosting parties for constituent groups, and doing volunteer work that sheds a favorable light on the college—are prime examples of these types of commitments. Extensive travel that keeps deans away from home also exacerbates the situation. For deans with children at home (especially those who are single parents), these time demands result in added pressures. Parents simply can't be at work and home at the same time. Important school events, such as basketball games and choir and band concerts, vie for slots on deans' calendars with meetings with potential donors, budgetary strategy sessions, and the like. As deans age and retire, a new generation will take their place. These deans are likely to have children living at home. Even if the average age of deans does not vary, we cannot assume that future deans will live in "child-free" homes. Today, more professionals, especially women, start families at an older age. This means that they enter leadership positions, such as the deanship, with children still in need of child care and parental involvement. In addition, parents are living longer, and they potentially represent another care-related issue for prospective deans. These future deans may be less able to strike work-life balances as well as current deans do (Glazer-Raymo, 1999; Wolverton, Wolverton & Gmelch 1999).

Study data (Table 8.6) suggest that female deans in particular may find it difficult to strike this balance. Even though all the deans, on average, were in their mid-fifties, significantly fewer female deans were married, and minority female deans were slightly less likely to be married than were their white female counterparts. Although more male deans had children still living at home, 27 percent of the women in the study assumed child-rearing responsibilities, and they experienced all related stressors to a greater extent than did the men. Over the past several decades, the presence of women in the workforce has grown. It appears, however, that job and societal norms remain such that many women in leadership positions find themselves unable to pursue both a marriage and a career.

How seductive it is to feel needed, to be crucial, to be praised, to know that what you do is important. For many self-driven deans, it takes little in-

Table 8.6
Family Status as It Relates to Personal and Professional Balance

	Married	Single	Children at Home
Male Deans	91%	9%	34%
Female Deans	68%*	32%	27%
Minority Deans	77%	23%	32%

*65% of minority females in the study were married.

stitutional prodding to push them into a perpetual state of disequilibrium. By succumbing to the wishes and desires of others, they unwittingly sacrifice their own personal integrity and wonder why their very full lives seem somehow incomplete (Wolverton, Wolverton, & Gmelch, 1999).

BALANCE FOR LESS EFFECTIVE DEANS

Because the Dean Morgans in this study believe they are effective, we can say little about deans who struggle in the position. We can, however, postulate that ineffective deans will improperly balance leadership and management. They may fail to place enough emphasis on leadership by paying equal attention to both, in effect not distinguishing between the two sets of responsibilities, or they may even weigh in too heavily on the side of management by relegating leadership to an administrative backburner. Furthermore, we suspect that either disposition will cause them to be less effective administrators. Since effective deans experience both scholarship-synergistic leadership and personal life–professional career imbalances, we can assume that ineffective deans are not immune to these pressures and indeed may suffer even greater imbalance in these areas and greater tensions than do effective deans.

LIFE AFTER THE DEANSHIP

One way to deal with imbalance is to redefine balance. Deans can do this by moving further into administration, moving away from administration, or leaving the academy. They reorient themselves by becoming provosts who are no longer expected to carry out research, by returning to faculty ranks where they no longer worry about the difference between management and leadership and instead concentrate on research and writing, or they leave by seeking employment outside higher education or by retiring.

Twenty-five percent or more of all deans in the study plan to return to their faculties, with fewer deans of nursing than of other colleges planning this career change (Table 8.7). Almost no one wanted to move to the same position at a similar institution, and liberal arts deans absolutely did not want to move outside the academy. (Education deans were slightly more likely to make a lateral move, and business deans were more apt to view nonacademic leadership as an option). A higher proportion of deans in liberal arts colleges (over one-third, compared to about one-fourth in the other colleges) saw provost or a comparable position as their next option.

A somewhat disturbing finding is that even though deans of nursing average more time in their positions (i.e., they have more experience) than do other deans, they are the least likely group to aspire to higher administrative positions. In fact, they are more apt than other deans to see retirement as their next move. Assuming that nursing deans understand the system and have performed well enough in it to survive longer than other deans, the loss of such talent may prove to be a higher education leadership drain.

Women tended to stay in current positions more often than men, and somewhat lower percentages of them plan to return to faculty positions or seek a higher administrative position (Table 8.8). Proportionally more minority deans plan to apply for upper administrative positions or return to faculty positions or retire than do their majority counterparts. Almost one-third of these deans plan to move to higher administrative positions, adding diversity to the upper levels of university leadership, but more than

Table 8.7
Life after the Deanship across Disciplines

Next Move	Liberal Arts	Business	Education	Nursing
Return to Faculty	.27	.24	.27	.18*
Deanship at Similar Institution	.04	.02	.07*	.03
Deanship at More Prestigious Institution	.08	.12	.08	.11
Higher Position in Academic Leadership	.35*	.26	.22*	.21*
Non-academic Leadership Position	.00*	.07*	.02	.05
No Interest in Moving	.15	.14	.17	.19
Retirement	.12*	.16	.17	.23*

*Indicates significant differences from all other deans

Table 8.8
Life after the Deanship

Next Move	Female Deans	Male Deans	Minority Deans
Return to Faculty	.22	.26	.27
Deanship at Similar Institution	.03	.06*	.01
Deanship at More Prestigious Institution	.10	.09	.05
Higher Position in Academic Leadership	.23	.28	.31
Non-academic Leadership Position	.04	.03	.05
No Interest in Moving	.19*	.14	.11
Retirement	.19	.15	.21

*Indicates significant differences from all other deans

25 percent plan to leave the academy for retirement or positions outside the academy, which suggests another potential leadership drain just as institutions are becoming more diverse.

IMPLICATIONS

In the search for balance, trade-offs become inevitable: more or less leadership coupled with more or less management, more or less scholarship, more or less professional life. The first relates to how they do their jobs; the second to how they define work priorities as they move from one profession to another; the third defines how they live life. In the first instance, it appears that highly effective deans purposefully trade off management for leadership. In the second and third instances, it appears that they grapple with the undesired results of attempting to trade synergistic leadership for scholarship and professional career for personal life. How these trade-offs get made may well determine the health and well-being of the deans and/or their colleges. Whether deans reach acceptable trade-offs may impact whether they remain in the deanship, take on other leadership roles, or leave administration entirely.

Thirty-four percent of deans view themselves as administrators. Highly effective deans are more apt to describe themselves as administrators, suggesting that a mental shift in self-perception away from faculty member to administrator helps deans to deal with balance issues. Those who rated themselves as moderately effective were less likely to describe themselves as administrators and more likely to think of themselves as a combination of faculty and administrator. Few in either group thought of themselves solely as academics. The question we might raise is: Do ineffective deans perceive themselves as academics? This possibility suggests that they would experience even greater imbalance between synergistic leadership and scholarship because of their predisposition toward scholarship and, perhaps, struggle more with the other two balancing acts as well.

A troublesome trend may be manifesting itself in the emerging propensity of women (especially in nursing) and minorities to leave the deanship and, possibly, the academy altogether. If they perceive themselves as effective, which they seem to do, we must ask ourselves why they are leaving. What is it about higher education that discourages these individuals from achieving balance and reaching their leadership potential? What detriment will their exodus be to higher education?

CHAPTER

Leadership Development: Answering the Call to Leadership

No one can deny that the Dean Morgans at colleges and universities across the country face multiple challenges. When asked to comment on the three greatest challenges they will face in the next three to five years, deans identified several hundred issues, from which seven categories emerged.

1. *Fiscal.* Budget and finance, allocating and using resources, internal and external fund-raising.
2. *Administration.* Working with top administration, long-range planning, reorganization, community outreach, public and legislative accountability.
3. *Program development.* Developing curricula and programs, recruiting high quality students, dealing with unprepared students.
4. *Faculty.* Recruiting and retaining faculty, dealing with difficult personnel, moving faculty toward change.
5. *Technology.* Distance learning, upgrading technology.
6. *Personal balance.* Balancing personal and professional lives, attaining personal goals.
7. *Diversity.* Ensuring diversity of faculty and student population.

More than 75 percent of the deans agreed that the fiscal, administration, and program development challenges were the three most important. Almost 30 percent of all respondents to this question rated fiscal challenges first. Twenty-six percent named administration as their first choice; 20 percent listed program development; about 14 percent chose faculty issues; fewer mentioned technology (5 percent), personal balance (3 percent), or diversity (≤ 2 percent) as top choices. Note: The small number of responses given with respect to diversity appears to indicate that the issue is either superseded in importance by others or that respondents believe that they are able to meet the challenge (Wolverton, Montez, & Gmelch, 2000).

Most of the challenges identified mirror the role dimensions discussed in chapter 4 (Table 9.1). The fiscal, administration, technology, and diversity challenges that deans anticipated correspond to the dimensions of external-political relations and resource management. The faculty challenge relates to the dimensions of internal productivity and academic personnel management. The challenge of program development relates directly to a unique variable originally included in the task inventory. The personal balance challenge that deans anticipated equates with the personal scholarship dimension. The only role dimension not readily identifiable in the challenge categories is leadership.

Comments such as "never have enough time," "frustrated at having others control much of my day," "limited resources and unlimited ambition make for high stress," and "not for the faint of heart" conjure up images of puppets on strings being pulled in multiple directions. We might raise the following questions: Do deans believe that the challenges they face will either expand or be redefined? Don't the demands associated with their current roles and future challenges suggest change? If so, doesn't constructive change require leadership? Are deans confident in their ability to lead, or are they simply responding as managers to these challenges, and not as leaders? In short, can all this be accomplished without leadership?

DEANS' LEADERSHIP DEVELOPMENT

Because many academic leaders first receive their training in their academic careers in research and teaching, they rarely anticipate the requirements of their current leadership positions, and thus they have had minimal management and leadership training (Hecht, Higgerson, Gmelch, & Tucker, 1999; Lucas, 1994, 2000). This is true in corporate cultures as well. The head of a large corporation once said, "We recruit people fresh out of college, and for thirty years we reward them for keeping their noses to the grindstone, doing their narrow jobs unquestionably. Then, when a top post opens up, we look around in frustration and say 'Where are the statesmen?' No one consciously intended to eliminate the statesman; but the organizational culture produced that result" (Gardner, 1987,

p. 19). We promulgate the same situation in higher education, socializing and rewarding our new Ph.D.s to become internationally renowned experts in narrow fields and then complain that no one is willing, or prepared, to be a generalist and serve in a leadership capacity.

Obstacles to Leadership Development

Why do some academics choose to lead and others not? What conditions do we create in higher education that act as barriers to attracting academics into leadership positions? Four come to mind.

Snuff out the spark before the leadership flame is ignited. First, institutions of higher education have themselves to blame. If a spark of enthusiasm for leadership is ignited in any of our young faculty, institutional systems may well snuff it out (Gardner, 1987). Far from encouraging faculty, we hold the need for discipline-specific experts and professionals higher than the need for leaders. In fact, many academics prefer an institution in which there are no leaders, only experts. Far from wishing to be leaders, faculty may conclude that they do not even want to associate with them. We fail to cultivate leadership talent in our junior faculty. We pay little attention to structuring academic leadership duties and opportunities in ways that make taking the position feasible. We offer few if any role models and provide little in the way of ongoing reinforcement and guidance in leadership skills and competencies.

Exalt the prestige and prowess of the professional expert. Second, some academics may possess the requisite skills and leadership ability but choose not to respond to the call (Boyatzis, 1990). The prestige of one's professional discipline drains off potential leaders into marvelously profitable nonleadership roles. From graduate school days on, institutions of higher education drive academics down the road to specialization.

"To mature as leaders, tomorrow's leaders must sooner or later climb out of the trenches of specialization and rise above the boundaries that separate the various segments of society" (Gardner, 1987, p. 7). Administrators must be generalists in order to cope with the diversity of problems and multitude of constituencies. They must be able to look at the academy with a broader vision and more systemic point of view.

Ignore the rigors of public and personal life. Third, many faculty have joined the academy in search of a professional life characterized by autonomy and independence. They observe the stormy years of deans and scathing criticisms of presidents and wonder "Why would I want to subject myself to such scrutiny and public criticism?" Today, personal privacy for deans does not exist. They are public servant leaders every moment of the day, with every appointment, message, and memo open to public scrutiny, critique,

Table 9.1
A Comparison of Current Roles and Future Challenges

Role Dimension	Future Challenges

External/political relations
  Funding
  Financial planning
  Build constituency involvement
  Promote diversity
  Ensure alumni support
  Represent college to administration
 	
Resource Management
  Proper recordkeeping
  Resource & nonacademic staff management
  Compliance with state, federal &
     certification agency guidelines
  Keep current with technological change
	Fiscal
	  Budget and finance
	  Allocation and use of resources
	  Internal and external fundraising
	
	Administration
	  Work with top administration
	  Long-range planning
	  Reorganization
	  Community outreach
	  Public/legislative accountability
	
	Technology
	  Distance learning
	  Upgrade technology
	
	Diversity
	  Ensure diversity of faculty and students

Internal Productivity
  Teaching
  Meet goals of the college
  Realize mission of the university
  Maintain healthy work environment
  Encourage faculty, chair & staff
     professional development activities
 	
Academic Personnel Management
  Recruit, select, and evaluate chairs
  Recruit, select, and evaluate faculty
	Faculty
	  Recruit and retain faculty
	  Deal with difficult personnel
	  Move faculty toward change

Personal Scholarship
  Maintain personal scholarship agenda
  Keep current in own discipline
  Demonstrate/model scholarship
	Personal Balance
	  Balance personal and professional lives
	  Attain personal goals

NO PARALLEL DIMENSION	Program development
	  Development of curricula and programs
	  Recruit high-quality students
	  Deal with unprepared students

Leadership
  Inform employees of univ/comm concerns
  Solicit ideas to improve the college
  Assign work
  Plan/conduct college leadership meetings
	NO PARALLEL CHALLENGE

comment, and review. Even at home, academics find that leadership is not a "family friendly" profession. Many academics are not willing to give up their professional and personal lives for one of servitude in the name of leadership.

Create a precarious state of executive selection. Finally, experts contend that the state of selection of the top three levels of the organization is precarious at best (Sessa & Taylor, 2000). In higher education, this includes presidents, provosts, and deans, although one might even question the state of selecting department chairpeople. Universities and colleges have very little expertise in the selection of executives and at times leave the process to executive search firms. When carried out in-house, untrained faculty and staff who look to replicate themselves rather than find someone with leadership skills distinct from their own make the selection. In short, most institutions of higher education have inadequate hiring, training, promotional, and succession-planning systems.

Recounting these obstacles is an attempt not to deafen any call to leadership but to point up the impediments we must overcome in order to develop our next generation of academic deans. How do we send out a call that will awaken latent leaders in the academy? How do we make some academics aware of their leadership potential? How do we make leadership feasible, tolerable, and inviting for academics?

THE DEVELOPMENT OF ACADEMIC LEADERS

The call to leadership in higher education occurs at a particular time. However, the success of a selection process cannot be gauged when the final decision is made and the offer accepted. How new deans are socialized into the college and how colleges adjust to their new deans are also central to a dean's success (Sessa & Taylor, 2000). Chapter 2 addressed how new deans manage the transition and socialization process—the expectations and anticipations before the first day in the position, the transition time into the position, and adjustment and stabilization for both the dean and the institution (Nicholson & West, 1989). Although it takes up to two and a half years to master the executive position (Gabarro, 1987), executive development does not stop there.

One of the most glaring shortcomings in the leadership area is the scarcity of sound research on the training and development of leaders (Conger & Benjamin, 1999). Gardner (1987) contends that leadership development is a process that extends over many years. Rather than search for answers in specific training programs, we suggest that three spheres of influence create the conditions essential to develop academic leaders: (a) conceptual understanding of the unique roles and responsibilities encompassed in academic leadership; (b) the skills necessary to achieve the results through working with faculty, staff, students, and other administrators; and (c) the practice of reflection to learn from past experiences and perfect the art of leadership. These three spheres and their intersections (Figure 9.1) serve as our analytical framework for what we believe is needed if we are to successfully develop effective leaders in the academy.[1]

Conceptual Understanding

Conceptual knowledge or understanding is the ability to conceptualize the leadership role of the dean. Cognitively, deans must explore and understand leadership by using mental models, frameworks, and role theory to reveal the many dimensions of leadership (Conger & Benjamin, 1999). Two issues are most important here: (a) as managers move into leadership positions, the concept of the job shifts; and (b) although some commonalities exist across all types of organizations, leaders in institutions of higher education face challenges not typical of managers and leaders in other organizations.

Figure 9.1
Dean Leadership Development

As academics move into the deanship from previous positions in the academy, they start to perceive themselves differently. For example, using Bolman and Deal's terms (1991), department chairpersons predominantly think in terms of their human and structural frames of leadership. As they move into the deanship, however, two new frames, the political and the symbolic, demand greater attention.

Second, the dimensions of leadership may be different, given the context and organizational conditions of the colleges and universities. Although the dean's roles may resemble those of other executives (Helgesen, 1990; Mintzberg, 1973), some are also peculiar to academe (Jackson, 2000). They serve the external and political relationships, manage college resources, promote internal productivity, attend to personnel matters, and engage in personal scholarship (see chapter 4). Roles, such as engaging in personal scholarship, are familiar, whereas others represent new responsibilities that deans accept when they move up the hierarchy.

Universities typically have taken the lead in teaching leadership to those outside the academy, particularly business executives through MBA programs, by imparting a conceptual understanding of the phenomenon. It is now time to teach academics what we know about leadership. Even though deans must ultimately define academic leadership for themselves, we suggest that a starting point might be the definition presented in Chapter 3. If one accepts this perspective of academic leadership, then what does it mean to build a community, empower others, and set direction?

Skill Development

Although a conceptual understanding of the deanship is a necessary condition to lead, it is insufficient without the application of appropriate behaviors and skills. Deans can formally learn to develop their leadership skills through clinical approaches, such as seminars, workshops, and lectures, then practice the principles through simulations, case studies, role playing, and action planning. Some skills—such as communication, performance coaching, conflict resolution, negotiation, and resource deployment—are more readily teachable than complex competencies such as strategic vision, which requires a long gestation period and involves a multiplicity of skills (Conger, 1992; Westley, 1992).

Many training opportunities for academic leaders are designed to have institutions send their mid-managers off-site for a general three- to four-day training program. These are effective in instilling key ingredients for skill development, but research has shown that it is more effective when work teams with their supervisors attend these programs because they support and reinforce each other's skill-building efforts (Conger, 1992).

Formal training is only one part of acquiring key skills. Although particular skills in and of themselves can be powerful, individuals often require on-the-job practical experience to translate skills from the intellectual level to a personal understanding that facilitates their application. According to a Chinese philosopher, to know and not to use is not yet to know. Experience is critical to skill building. It also takes various experiences: experimenting, receiving feedback, coaching, refining, and perfecting (Ericsson & Smith, 1991).

Reflective Practice

Leadership development is an inner journey. Self-knowledge, personal awareness, and corrective feedback must be part of a dean's leadership journey, and moral, ethical, and spiritual dimensions are necessary to complete the trek. Leadership development is very much about finding one's voice (Kouzes & Posner, 1987; Matusak, 1997). Because credibility and authenticity lie at the heart of leadership, the ability to determine one's own guiding beliefs and assumptions undergirds effective leadership. By providing structured feedback, promoting reflection, and developing self-awareness we can create conditions for the reflective executive to flourish.

Donald Schön, in his book *The Reflective Practitioner* (1983), asks, What is the kind of knowing in which competent practitioners engage? We can begin with the assumption that competent practitioners know more than they say and that they exhibit a kind of knowing-in-practice, most of which is tacit. Times change, as do constructs and the skills needed to lead. This calls for the art of practice, which might be taught if it were constant and known, but it is not. Schön contends that reflection-in-action is central to dealing well with uncertainty, instability, uniqueness, and value conflict—common occurrences in deans' leadership lives.

For this reason alone, the use of reflection-in-action is critically important. We must develop strategies for reflection that place technical problem solving within the broader context of reflective inquiry. Deans' isolation in their respective positions works against reflection-in-action. Schön suggests, "Managers do reflect-in-action, but they seldom reflect on their reflection-in-action. Hence, this crucially important dimension of their art tends to remain private and inaccessible to others. Moreover, because awareness of one's intuitive thinking usually grows out of practice in articulating it to others, managers often have little access to their own reflection-in-action" (p. 243). As a result, deans need to communicate their private dilemmas and insights and to test them against the views of their peers. Leadership development does not take place within a vacuum

(Beineke & Sublett, 1999). Its nurturing flourishes best within a group or with trusted colleagues acting as mentors, partners, and coaches.

In sum, leadership development must incorporate all three approaches: conceptual development, skill building, and reflective practice. Each integrates and builds upon the other. The development of leadership rests with the receptiveness of organizations to support and coach such skills. It does, however, depend on the individual's own motivation and talent. In part, leadership is passion, and you cannot teach people to be passionate.

RECOMMENDATIONS

In the final section, we highlight strategies that can foster dean leadership development. Table 9.2 provides a visual display of these strategies. We have grouped them under the three components of leadership development—conceptual understanding, skill development, and reflective practice—and across three levels of interventions—personal, institutional, and professional.

Conceptual Understanding

At the **personal** level, deans can expand their conceptual understanding of the position by enrolling in classes that deal with specific higher education administration topics, such as budgeting and finance, planning, and current issues. They can also read the *Chronicle of Higher Education, Change* magazine, and other periodicals that target higher education audiences. In addition, they can attend conferences, such as the American Association for Higher Education (AAHE) and the American Association of Colleges and Universities (AACU), which feature presentations, workshops, and symposia on higher education administration. On their own campuses, they can "partner" with other deans to form a support network to discuss professional as well as personal issues of deaning. These efforts can aid deans in gaining a better grasp on how others go about balancing management with leadership, scholarship with leadership, and their personal and professional lives.

Institutions can define the scope of the job through systemic efforts, and seamless approaches to the selection, socialization, and development of deans. These programs might include retreats and orientation programs. For example, in its systemic effort, the Iowa State University formed a collaborative, the Academic Leadership Forum, which is inclusive of all the deans and department chairpeople in the colleges of education, engineering, and business. They collectively developed monthly academic agendas for the entire year around leadership topics such as change management,

Table 9.2
Strategies for Dean Leadership Development

Strategies for Dean Development	Leadership Development Component			
Levels of Intervention	Conceptual Understanding	Skill Development	Reflective Practice	
Personal	Classes on higher education Readings (*Chronicle of Higher Education*; *Change* magazine) AAHE; AACU Conferences Partner deans	External seminars (ACE; AAHE) Center for Leadership Effectiveness Executive MBA/MPA	Select mentor/guide Journal writing Networking Coaching	
Institutional	Academic Leadership Forum Seamless selection, socialization, & development Dean retreats Orientation Program	Academic Leadership Forum In-house workshops/seminars Exchanges Internships & Shadowing	Academic Leadership Forum Academic Partnerships Structure dean working councils Mentor program	
Professional	Quondam Dean Academy New Deans Institute Dean Associations Create cadre of academic leaders Rethink the position	AACTE AACSB CCAS AACN Conference workshops Annual meetings Publications	Internet networks Consortia Regional, State, Systems Networks	

visioning, faculty development, and strategic thinking. In addition, each dean and department chairperson is teamed with another from a different college to form a Partner in Academic Leadership (PAL). These pairs meet twice a month informally to discuss topics, share what is going well and what is getting in the way, and talk about how they might approach their jobs differently. The success of this type of institutional program is dependent on some key design elements: (a) a single well-delineated leadership model, such as Figure 9.1; (b) extended learning periods—from an initial intensive year-long program to continuous learning in the subsequent years; (c) monthly sessions centered on topics identified by participants; (d) a cohort system (PALs); (5) PAL assignment of a joint task to be completed, such as leading a Forum training session; and (6) the involvement of the entire academic leadership team from each participating college.

A seamless process would incorporate training across all phases of dean acclimation. Prior to assuming the deanship (or very early in a new dean's tenure) universities need to systematically invest in and formally train the future leaders of their institutions. They need to think about "growing" their own deans, cultivating promising academic leaders, spotting them early on in their academic careers as faculty. They need to prepare these potential leaders in such areas as conflict resolution, fund-raising, personnel management, time and stress management, change facilitation and management, team work, delegation, mentoring, planning and visioning, and budgeting and fiscal management. This task need not be as difficult as it might seem. For example, the Academic Leadership Forum mentioned above contains some of these elements. As a supplement, many universities house MBA programs. Some of the skills necessary for running a college are the same as for operating a business, so why not create an MBA for academics?

During the deanship, universities must provide for continued professional leadership development. In-house retreats with the provost and president go a long way toward educating deans about their particular institutions. In addition, a professional development allowance provides deans with the time and money to take advantage of workshops, seminars, and intensive leadership development programs offered elsewhere. Similarly, provisions for periodic renewal, such as professional leaves after five years of service, provide a break from the pressures of the position and further opportunity to pursue professional development. Such leaves could be used to promote the continued capacity of the individual as dean or to help him or her prepare to return to the faculty or move to another administrative position.

Professional organizations, such as AAHE and the American Council on Education (ACE), provide excellent conferences and forums to explore strategic issues in the academy. In addition, the disciplinary-specific professional organization, the American Association of Colleges for Teacher Education (AACTE), sponsors a weeklong New Deans' Institute to orient newly appointed education deans into their positions. Within AACTE, deans from similar institutions have also formed separate organizations (land grant deans, comprehensive university deans, and liberal arts college deans) to further their discussions and address common problems. Organizations such as the Council for Colleges of Arts and Sciences (CCAS) and the American Assembly of Collegiate Schools of Business (AACSB) also provide conferences and institutes to socialize their deans into their leadership positions.

When deans move out of the dean's role, they can themselves play a part in training future generations of academic leaders by mentoring, counseling, and teaching those new to the endeavor. Retired or former deans have been through the rites of passage and are key resources for the socialization and success of the next generation of deans. These quondam deans, if organized into an academy, could provide an invaluable resource to colleges and universities for developing leadership capacity in institutions of higher education. A Quondam Dean Academy could be used both for training purposes and forming a cadre of executives-on-loan that serve in interim positions. In the first instance, successful former deans conceptually understand the institutions and roles and responsibilities and could aid new deans as they transition into the position. In the second, when a college needs cleaning up and a new dean would have to burn too many bridges to do the job, a quondam dean could come in on hazardous duty, so to speak, to do the dirty work, leaving the college in good shape for a new incoming permanent dean.

Finally, rethinking the position in a manner that alters its conceptual understanding may broaden the appeal of the deanship. Currently, many deanships reflect a traditional hierarchical structure: the dean at the top, with associate deans clearly relegated to subordinate positions. Professional organizations might begin a dialogue about the merit of such power delineation and how it impacts the ability of deans to establish balance. Considering the concept of shared leadership can serve as a starting point. Its general premises—shared responsibility, a tangible vision, mutual influence, and a bias for action—seem directed at moving the concept of leadership from a person-centered to a team-based philosophy (Astin, 1996; Astin & Astin, 1996; Yukl, 1998). A leadership team might comprise "a small number of people with complementary skills who are committed to common purposes, performance goals, and leadership approaches for which they hold themselves mutually accountable. . . . Team performance at the top is all about doing work together, about collective action. [In such situations] real work [goes beyond] open discussion, debate, decision making, and delegation of authority" (Katzenbach, 1998, pp. 111, 217). These leadership teams can run the gamut from a dean who delegates a great deal of power and authority to associate deans, but still remains the sole leader at the top, to partnerships at the top in which two or more deans work and lead in tandem to accomplish the mission of the college.

Skill Development

The skills that department chairpersons and deans acquire in their ascension to the deanship are not always adequate or appropriate for deans. Deans often deal in the political and symbolic frames of leadership and need to develop new skills to be successful in their jobs. A **personal** development plan starts with an assessment of the match between the types of skills deans bring to their jobs and the demands of their positions. Deans unfamiliar with managerial subtleties need to seek out opportunities to hone their executive skills. The professional development market is replete with commercial venues for management seminars, from performance coaching to principled negotiation. These individual programs tend to be relatively short, from half-day seminars to a few days or weeks, but with little or no follow-up. Not so abundant are skill development programs tailor-made for academic leaders. Professional education organizations, such as ACE, AACU, and AAHE, sponsor seminars and preconference workshops on a variety of topics with the primary goal of imparting knowledge and initial skill development to enhance leadership performance. Other more extensive leadership development programs (two or more weeks) are available to deans through such organizations and institutions as the Center for Creative Leadership, Harvard's Management Development Program (MDP), Stanford's Executive Development Program, and Bryn Mawr's program for female academic leaders. Executive MBA programs offer a more systemic approach to intensive skill attainment but require a greater commitment of a dean's time and resources.

Institutions can encourage this type of professional development through their offices of human resource development. They typically provide in-house workshops and seminars that focus on real-life leadership and campus issues. Most programs, however, are designed for mid-management and address more managerial issues, personnel practices, legal issues, and budget development, for instance, than difficult leadership and ethical dilemmas often plaguing deans. Instead, year-long and continuous professional development programs, such as the Academic Leadership Forum mentioned earlier, stimulate and sustain skill development through practice and reinforcement of key executive skills. Finally, institutions can promote executive internships and exchanges across colleges and across industries.

Internships, shadowing experiences, and exchanges could be developed by universities to facilitate skill acquisition. Ewell (1999) suggests that "adopting" a management technique or effective leadership plan is quite different from actually, learning how to use it and then practicing it. When attempting to learn and develop technical skills, such as working with diverse populations, fiscal and resource management, and strategic planning, deans may find that functioning in a foreign work environment provides useful insights. Shadowing experiences, in which deans partner with other executives, be it at another college, at a university, or with a corporate partner, could constitute professional development sabbaticals of various lengths, from one week to one year. They could be short intensive exercises or longer and regular, but intermittent, in nature (Wolverton & Poch, 2000).

Shadowing experiences can also be described as "executives on loan," and when they are, they become leadership exchanges. Such exchanges are not a new idea. Pulling (1989) advocated collaborative leadership arrangements. The benefits of these exchanges merit some discussion. New deans need to be prepared for fund-raising and for personnel, time, stress, and fiscal management (Gmelch et al., 1999). However, few deans receive basic training that helps them to sift through the "administrivia" and focus on important issues. Experienced deans and business CEOs who are highly effective at what they do often possess analytical skills, such as cost-cutting strategies, outsourcing, and training a transient workforce, that deans need if their colleges are to run smoothly (English, 1992; van der Werf, 1999).

Professional organizations, including the AACTE, the CCAS, the AACSB, and the American Association of Colleges of Nursing (AACN), also share the responsibility for ensuring that deans are proficient in what they do. Deans who maintain active membership in broad-based higher education professional organizations reap the benefit of learning more generalized approaches to academic leadership than they once received from their specialized discipline-centered professional organizations. Although deans, like faculty, are most concerned about keeping current with their disciplines, leadership now has become the discipline within which deans must hone their skills. From the general higher education associations' annual meetings, publications, and networks, deans can learn the language, literature, and innovations of higher education (Green & McDade, 1994).

Reflective Practice

Reflective practice remains one of the more illusive components of leadership development. It takes far more time and must be ongoing over long periods of time. Deans can engage in networking and seek mentoring and coaching. Each of these types of interaction provides for immediate feedback, advice, and support. Perhaps, the most reflective and **personal** activity in which deans can engage is through journal writing, personal dictation, or other means of reflecting and imprinting one's professional experience. In a qualitative study of the socialization of one new dean, the subject kept a personal diary by ending each day dictating responses to three questions: What went well? What got in the way? What would I do different the next time? Leaders need to find their own way through their reflective practice. In the end, such practice helps deans to prioritize and weigh their professional careers against their personal lives.

Institutions that put in place formal structures, such as the Academic Leadership Forum, academic partnerships, working councils, and mentoring programs, provide their deans with systematic means to formative evaluation and mechanisms through which they can seek to improve themselves. Literature on mentoring and partner programs suggests that professional organizations have reservations because they demand too much time, afford chances for exploitation or dependency, or are simply neither wanted nor needed. However, such institutional support programs have been shown to provide mutual psychological support, increase chances of creativity, furnish support for information and action plans, enhance learning from each other, and provide structured time for reflection (Boice, 1992; Conger, 1992). The PAL program at Iowa State University pairs deans and chairpeople with like positions across colleges. In their bimonthly meetings, they share their experiences and readings, attend and discuss seminars, and plan a skill development session for the entire leadership group of twenty-six deans and chairpersons. Their testimonials speak to the benefit of having a confidant outside the department and college, learning from other's perspectives, and supportively bonding during times of ethical and moral dilemmas (Gmelch, 2000b).

In addition to partnering relationships, mentoring helps newcomers to acclimate to their environments and work. It offers an opportunity for a novice to "learn the ropes" of an organization with which he or she is unfamiliar. Too often, however, formal mentoring for leadership succession is reserved for a select few. The following situation illustrates the case in point: Despite the growth of female CEOs in the past years, only 2 to 3 percent of the largest companies have female CEOs. When asked why, male

CEOs thought that lack of experience accounted for the low numbers. In contrast, the female executives cited inhospitable and exclusionary attitudes and patterns (including a lack of effective mentoring) that kept them from top positions (Wah, 1998).

Such differences of opinion cross academic-business borders and suggest that even though mentorships may be well intentioned, they can be misdirected. One solution to the dilemma might lie in training potential mentors in order to sensitize them to issues specific to women and minorities (Oakes, 1999; Thomas & Gabarro, 1999). Within institutions and even across universities some distance from each other, deans prepared to mentor could sponsor and shepherd new deans through their beginning years. Another solution might entail breaking with the tradition that business executives mentor other executives and academics mentor deans. Cross-mentorships, in which academics advise executives and CEOs help to prepare deans, could produce unexpected and profitable results in much the same way that cross-fertilization in plants does.

Finally, **professional** organizations can help deans to establish networks. Through attending national conferences and professional development programs, deans get connected with their colleagues, form personal relationships, and develop networks of confidants. Like the freshman experience in college, freshmen deans attending AACTE's New Deans' Institute form a collegial support group that bonds during the meeting and stays connected electronically throughout the year until the next conference they attend in common. Green and McDade (1994) also reported deans' "high satisfaction with consortia, regional and state networks, and system networks that bring together deans from peer and geographically linked institutions" (p. 109). By helping deans across institutions, states, and countries consider what it is they really do, how they do it, and why they do it, professional organizations go a long way toward guaranteeing effective leadership.

THE CALL TO LEADERSHIP

The transformation from faculty to academic leadership takes time and dedication, and not all academics successfully make the complete transition to leadership. This book has examined the personal challenges that academics must surmount if they are to respond successfully to the call for one specific form of academic leadership, the deanship. Deans typically come to the position without prior executive experience (chapters 2 and 7), without knowing what is meant by academic leadership (chapter 3), without a clear understanding of the ambiguity and complexity of their roles (chapter 4), without knowing the commitment required to lead a college (chapter 6), without recognition of the metamorphic changes that occur as one transforms from an academic to an administrative leader (chapter 2), without an awareness of the stress and cost to their academic and personal lives (chapters 5 and 8), and without sufficient leadership preparation and training (chapter 9).

The Call without Administrative Experience

Deans serve an average of six years. Opportunities for individual skill development through training are woefully inadequate. Even with systematic skill development opportunities available, if you ask managers where they learned their leadership abilities, most will say from their job experiences. In fact, a poll of 1,450 managers from twelve corporations cited experience, not the classroom, as the best preparation for leadership (Ready, 1994). We should not conclude, however, that formal training and education are of limited value. Academic leadership training, in combination with experience and socialization, can heighten an appreciation for leadership and strengthen one's motivation to develop leadership capabilities.

The Call without Understanding the Duality of the Position

Caught between conflicting interests of faculty and administration, trying to look in two directions, academic leaders often do not know which way to turn (Hecht et al., 1999; Lucas, 1994, 2000). Deans promote the university mission to faculty and, at the same time, champion the values of their faculty. As a result, they find themselves swiveling between their faculty colleagues and university administration. In essence, their persona becomes Janus-like; they must look in two directions at the same time. Academic leaders do not have to worry about being deified, but they do find themselves in a unique position—a leadership role that has no parallel in business or industry (Gmelch & Miskin, 1993, 1995). To balance their roles they must learn to swivel without appearing dizzy, schizophrenic, or "two-faced." They must employ a facilitative leadership style while working with faculty in the academic core and a more traditional authoritative style with the administrative core.

The Call without Knowing the Stress the Job Entails

Behind the achievements of many great deans lies the factor of stress: not necessarily distress (negative stress), but the eustress (positive stress) of success. Deans tend to thrive on challenges and are drawn into the seduction of success. However, as explored in chapter 5, deans also experience stress from administrative tasks, working with the provost, fund-raising, faculty relations, and the pressures of time. After all, they can only put out so many brush fires, deal with so many constituencies, and mediate so many faculty conflicts without being on the verge of burnout. Deans seem to sustain life on the edge, but over time they need to find balance and recognize that they cannot do everything.

The Call without an Awareness of the Cost to Scholarship

One of the greatest dilemmas for deans revolves around trying to hold on to their faculty identity (Tucker & Bryan, 1988). Many academic leaders are torn between trying to teach and be a leader, conduct research and be a leader, or teach and research and be an effective leader. Only geniuses can do all three. Not surprisingly, with sixteen years of socialization in their discipline before entering administration, many deans feel most comfortable and competent in their scholar role. Most deans would spend more time on their own academic endeavors if they could, but they find it virtually impossible because of the demands of administrative duties.

The Call without Leadership Development

To become an expert takes time. Studies of executives in the corporate world who attain international levels of performance point to the ten-year rule of preparation (Ericsson, Drampe, & Tesch-Romer, 1993). In the American university, seven years represents the threshold for faculty to attain the status of expert and achieve tenure and promotion at the associate professor level, and another seven years to attain full membership in the academy. If it takes seven to fourteen years to achieve expertise in our academic disciplines, why do we assume that we can create academic leaders with weekend seminars?

Today, as never before, higher education needs competent leaders. As deans move from academically intense faculty and department chairperson positions, many make conscious career choices that catapult them into the arena of upper-level administration and leadership. Some even move on to become provosts and presidents, making the deanship a primary leadership training ground. The lines of succession seem fairly clear, but the relatively high turnover rates of deans, provosts, and presidents suggest that we do not groom our leaders in ways that promote longevity, success, and effectiveness in higher education leadership (Korschgen, Fuller, & Gardner, 2001). For this reason alone, higher education can ill afford the luxury of almost total inattention when it comes to preparing deans for this and other future leadership responsibilities.

NOTE

1. Jay Conger, in his book *Learning to Lead* (1992), approached his study of leadership development from a training perspective—identifying and investigating the five best innovative leadership programs in North America. We have focused on the key components that individuals need if they are to develop as leaders. Although both approaches are similar, our approach to leadership development is subtly different. From Conger's perspective, deans receive training through others' overt actions, whereas we believe that personal development starts from within—a "leader-centered" approach.

REFERENCES

Abdel-Halim, A. (1981). Effects of role stress-job design-technology interaction on employee work satisfaction. *Academy of Management Journal, 24,* 260–273.

Abraham, R. (1999). The impact of emotional dissonance on organizational commitment and intention to turnover. *Journal of Psychology, 133*(4), 441–455.

Allen, K. E., & Cherrey, C. (2000). *Systemic leadership: Enriching the meaning of our work.* Lanham, MD: University Press of America.

Allen, N. J., & Meyer, J. P. (1996). Affective, continuance, and normative commitment to the organization: An examination of construct validity. *Journal of Vocational Behavior, 49,* 252–276.

Association of Governing Boards of Universities and Colleges. (1996). Ten public policy issues for higher education in 1996. Washington, DC: Association of Governing Boards of Universities and Colleges.

Assouline, M., & Meir, E. (1987). Meta-analysis of the relationship between congruence and well-being measures. *Journal of Vocational Behavior, 31,* 319–332.

Astin, A. (1993). *What matters in college? Four critical years revisited.* San Francisco: Jossey-Bass.

Astin, A., & Astin, H. (2001, January). Principles of transformative leadership. *AAHE Bulletin, 53*(5), 3–6,16.

Astin, H. (1996, July/August). Leadership for social change. *About Campus,* 4–10.

Astin, H., & Astin, A. W. (1996). *A social change model of leadership development guidebook*. Los Angeles: UCLA Higher Education Research Institute.

Astin, H., & Leland, C. (1991). *Women of influence: Women of vision*. San Francisco: Jossey-Bass.

Atchinson, T. J., & Lefferts, E. A. (1972). The prediction of turnover using Herzberg's job satisfaction technique. *Personnel Psychology, 25*, 53–64.

Austin, A. E. (1984). The work experience of university and college administrators. *American Association of University Administrators, 6*(1), 1–6.

Austin, A. E. (1985a). *Factors contributing to job satisfaction of university mid-level administrators*. Paper presented at ASHE Conference, Chicago.

Austin, A. E. (1985b). *University mid-level administrators: Comparisons between men and women on work experience, commitment, and job satisfaction*. Paper presented at AERA Conference, Chicago.

Austin, A. E., & Rice, R. E. (1998). Making tenure viable: Listening to early career faculty. *American Behavioral Scientist 41*(5), 736–754.

Bailey, F. G. (1988). *Humbuggery and manipulation: The art of leadership*. Ithaca, NY: Cornell University Press.

Bailyn, L. (1989). Toward the perfect workplace? *Communications of the ACM 32*, 460–471.

Bailyn, L. (1993). *Breaking the mold: Women, men, and time in the new corporate world*. New York: Free Press.

Bailyn, L., Fletcher, J. K., & Kolb, D. (1997). Unexpected connections: Considering employees' personal lives can revitalize your business. *Sloan Management Review*, 11–19.

Baker, W. J., & Gloster, A., II. (1994). Moving toward the virtual university: A vision of technology in higher education. *Cause/Effect, 17*, 4–11.

Baldridge, J. V. (1971). *Power & conflict in the university: Research in the sociology of complex organizations*. New York: Wiley.

Balfour, D. L., & Wechsler, B. (1990). Organizational commitment: A reconceptualization and empirical test of public-private differences. *Review of Public Personnel Administration, 10*(3), 23–40.

Bandura, A. (1986). *Social foundations of thought and action: A social-cognitive view*. Englewood Cliffs, NJ: Prentice Hall.

Banks, C.A.M. (1995). Gender and race as factors in educational leadership and administration. In J. Banks, & C.A.M. Banks (Eds.), *Handbook of research on multicultural education* (pp. 65–80). New York: Macmillan.

Bartel, A. P. (1981). Race differences in job satisfaction: A reappraisal. *Journal of Human Resources, 16*, 295–303.

Bass, B. M. (1985). *Leadership and performance beyond expectations*. New York: Free Press.

Bass, B. M. (1990). *Handbook of leadership: A survey of theory and research*. New York: Free Press.

Bass, B. M. (1998). *Transformational leadership: Industrial, military and educational impact*. Mahwah, NJ: Erlbaum.

Bateman, T. S., & Strasser, S. (1983). A cross-lagged regression test of the relationship between job tension and employee satisfaction. *Journal of Applied Psychology, 68*(3), 439–445.

Bates, F. L. (1956). Position, role, and status: A reformulation of concepts. *Social Forces, 34*, 313–321.

Becker, T. E. (1992). Foci and bases of commitment: Are they distinctions worth making? *Academy of Management Journal, 335*, 232–244.

Becker, T. E., Billings, R. S., Eveleth, D. M., & Gilbert, N. L. (1996). Foci and bases of employee commitment: Implications for job performance. *Academy of Management Journal, 39*, 464–482.

Bedeian, A., & Armenakis, A. (1981). A path-analytic study of the consequences of role conflict and role ambiguity. *Academy of Management Journal, 24*, 417–424.

Beineke, J. A., & Sublett, R. H. (1999). *Leadership lessons and competencies: Learning from the Kellogg National Fellowship Program*. Battle Creek, MI: Kellogg Foundation.

Belenky, M. F., Clinchy, B. M., Goldberger, N. R., & Tarule, J. M. (1986). *Women's ways of knowing: The development of self, voice, and mind*. New York: Basic Books.

Bell, E. E., & Nkomo, S. M. (1998). *Our separate ways*. New York: Doubleday.

Bennett, C. I. (1995). Research on racial issues in American higher education. In J. Banks, & C.A.M. Banks (Eds.), *Handbook of research on multicultural education* (pp. 663–682). New York: Macmillan.

Bennett, S. M., & Shayner, J. A. (1988). The role of senior administration in women's leadership development. In M. Sagaria (Ed.), *Empowering women: Leadership development strategies on campus* (pp. 27–38). San Francisco: Jossey-Bass.

Bennis, W. (1999). *Managing people is like herding cats*. Provo, UT: Executive Excellence.

Bennis, W. G., & Nanus, B. (1985). *Leaders: The strategies for taking charge*. New York: Harper & Row.

Bensimon, E. M., Neumann, A., & Birnbaum, R. (1989). *Making sense of administrative leadership: The "L" word in higher education* (AAHE-ERIC Higher Education Report No. 1). Washington, DC: George Washington University.

Bergin, M., & Solman, R. (1988). Perceptions of role related stress in senior educational executives and its relationship to their health. *Journal of Educational Administration, 26*, 159–183.

Biddle, B. J. (1979). *Role theory: Expectations, identities, and behaviors*. New York: Academic Press.

Biddle, B. J., & Thomas, E. (Eds.). (1966). *Role theory: Concepts and research*. New York: Wiley.

Biglan, A. (1973). The characteristics of subject matter in different academic areas. *Journal of Applied Psychology, 57,* 195–203.

Birnbaum, R. (1990). *How colleges work: The cybernetics of academic organization and leadership.* San Francisco: Jossey-Bass.

Blau, G. (1981). An empirical investigation of job stress, social support, service length, and job strength. *Organizational Behavior and Human Performance, 27,* 279–302.

Blix, A. G., & Lee, J. W. (1991). Occupational stress among university administrators. *Research in Higher Education, 32*(3), 289–302.

Blood, R. E. (1966). *The functions of experience in professional preparation: Teaching and the principalship.* Unpublished doctoral dissertation, Claremont Graduate School, Claremont, California.

Bluedorn, A. C. (1982). A unified model of turnover from organizations. *Human Relations, 35,* 135–153.

Boice, R. (1992). Lessons learned about mentoring. In M. D. Sorcinelli & A. E. Austin (Eds.), *Developing new and junior faculty* (pp. 51–62). San Francisco: Jossey-Bass.

Bolman, L. G., & Deal, T. E. (1991). *Reframing organizations.* San Francisco: Jossey-Bass.

Boone, L. E., Kurtz, D. L., & Fleenor, C. P. (1988). The road to the top. *American Demographics,* 31–37.

Booth, D. B. (1982). *The department chair: Professional development and role conflict* (AAHE-ERIC Higher Education Research Report No. 10). Washington, DC: AAHE.

Bowditch, J. L., & Buono, A. F. (1997). *A primer on organizational behavior* (4th ed.). New York: Wiley.

Boyatzis, R. (1990). *Beyond competence: The choice to be a leader.* Paper presented at the Academy of Management Meetings, San Francisco.

Braddock, J. H., & McPartland, J. M. (1987). How minorities continue to be excluded from equal employment opportunities: Research on labor market and institutional barriers. *Journal of Social Issues, 43*(1), 5–39.

Brewer, K. C. (1995). *The stress management handbook: A practical guide to reducing stress in every aspect of your life.* Shawnee Mission, KS: National Press Publications.

Bridges, W. (1980). *Transitions: Making sense of life's changes.* Reading, MA: Addison-Wesley.

Bridges, W. (1991). *Managing transitions.* Reading, MA: Perseus Books.

Brooke, P. P., Jr., Russell, D. W., & Price, J. L. (1988). Discriminant validation of measures of job satisfaction, job involvement, and organizational commitment. *Journal of Applied Psychology, 73*(2), 139–145.

Brown, S. (1988). *Increasing minority faculty: An elusive goal.* Princeton, NJ: Educational Testing Service.

Burns, J. M. (1978). *Leadership.* New York: Harper & Row.

Butler, J. E., & Walter, J. C. (Eds.). (1991). *Transforming the curriculum: Ethnic studies and women's studies*. Albany: State University of New York Press.

California Higher Education Policy Center. (1994). *Three strikes could undermine college opportunity*. San Jose, CA: ERIC. (ED 406 937)

Cannon, W. B. (1939). *The wisdom of the body*. New York: Norton.

Caplan, R. D. (1983). Person–environment fit: Past, present, and future. In C. L. Cooper (Ed.), *Stress research* (pp. 35–78). New York: Wiley.

Caplan, R. D., Cobb, S., French, J.R.P., Van Harrison, R., & Pinneau, S. R. (1980). *Job demands and worker health: Main effects and occupational differences*. Ann Arbor, MI: University of Michigan.

Carnegie Foundation for the Advancement of Teaching. (1990). *Campus life: In search of community*. Princeton, NJ: Carnegie Foundation.

Carr, D., Hard, K., & Trahant, W. (1996). *Managing the change process: A field guide for change agents, consultants, team leaders and reengineering managers*. New York: McGraw-Hill.

Carroll, A. B. (1974). Role conflict in academic organizations: An exploratory examination of the department chair's experience. *Educational Administration Quarterly 10(2)*, 51–64.

Carroll, J. B. (1991). Career paths of department chairs: A national perspective. *Research in Higher Education, 32(6)*, 669–686.

Chliwniak, L. (1997). *Higher education leadership: Analyzing the gender gap* (ASHE-ERIC Higher Education Report No. 4). Washington, DC: George Washington University. Graduate School of Education and Human Development.

Clark, A. E., & Oswald, A. J. (1996). Satisfaction and comparison income. *Journal of Public Economics, 61*, 359–381.

Clugston, M. (2000). The mediating effects of multidimensional commitment on job satisfaction and intent to leave. *Journal of Organizational Behavior, 21(4)*, 477–486.

Conger, J. A. (1992). *Learning to lead: The art of transforming managers into leaders*. San Francisco: Jossey-Bass.

Conger, J. A., & Benjamin, B. (1999). *Building leaders: How successful companies develop the next generation*. San Francisco: Jossey-Bass.

Cook, J., & Wall, T. (1980). New work attitude measures of trust, organizational commitment and personal need non-fulfillment. *Journal of Occupational Psychology, 53*, 39–52.

Cooper, B. S., Sieverding, J. W., & Muth, R. (1988). Principals' management behavior, personality types and physiological stress. *Journal of Educational Administration, 2*, 197–221.

Cosgrove, D. (1986). *The effects of principal succession on elementary schools*. Unpublished doctoral dissertation, University of Utah, Salt Lake City.

Coughlan, W. D. (1994). The balance of a lifetime. *Association Management, 46(1)*, 66–73.

Cox, T., Jr. (1994). *Cultural diversity in organizations: Theory, research and practice.* San Francisco: Berrett-Koehler.

Cox T. A., & Harquail, C. V. (1991). Career paths and career success in the early career of male and female MBAs. *Journal of Vocational Behavior, 39,* 54–75.

Creswell, J. W., & England, M. E. (1994). Improving informational resources for academic deans and chairpersons. In M. K. Kinnick (Ed.), *Providing useful information for deans and department chairs* (pp. 5–18). San Francisco: Jossey-Bass.

Creswell, J. W., Wheeler, D. W., Seagren, A. T., Egly, N. Y., & Beyer, K. D. (1990). *The academic chairperson's handbook.* Lincoln, NE: University of Nebraska Press.

Cronin, B., & Crawford, H. (1999). Do deans publish what they preach? *Journal of the American Society for Information Science, 50*(5), 471–474.

Cyphert, F. R., & Zimpher, N. L. (1980). The education deanship: Who is the dean? In D. E. Griffiths & D. J. McCarty (Eds.), *The dilemma of the deanship* (pp. 91–122). Danville, IL: Interstate.

Dawis, R. V. (1994). The theory of work adjustment as convergent theory. In M. L. Savickas & P. W. Lent (Eds.), *Convergence in career development theories: Implications for science and practice* (pp. 33–43). Palo Alto, CA: Consulting Psychologists.

Dawis, R. V., England, G. W., & Lofquist, L. H. (1964). *A theory of work adjustment* (Vol. 15). Minneapolis: University of Minnesota. Industrial Resource Center.

Dawis, R. V., & Lofquist, L. H. (1984). *A psychological theory of work adjustment.* Minneapolis: University of Minnesota.

Day, D. V., & Bedeian, A. G. (1995). Personality similarity and work-related outcomes among African-American nursing personnel: A test of the supplemental model of person-environment congruence. *Journal of Vocational Behavior, 46,* 55–70.

DeConinck, J. B., Stilwell, C. D., & Brock, B. A. (1996). A construct validity analysis of scores on measures of distributive justice and pay satisfaction. *Educational and Psychological Measurement, 56,* 1026–1036.

DePree, M. (1992). *Leadership jazz.* New York: Dell.

Dibden, A. J. (Ed.). (1968). *The academic deanship in American colleges and universities.* Carbondale, IL: Southern Illinois University Press.

Diener, E., Emmons, R. A., Larsen, R. J., & Griffin, S. (1985). The satisfaction with life scale. *Journal of Personality Assessment, 49,* 71–75.

Dill, W. R. (1980). The deanship: An unstable craft. In D. E. Griffiths & D. J. McCarty (Eds.), *The dilemma of the deanship* (pp. 261–284). Danville, IL: Interstate.

Dupont, G. E. (1968). The dean and his office. In A. J. Dibden (Ed.), *The academic deanship in American colleges and universities.* Carbondale: Southern Illinois University Press.

Eby, L. T., Freeman, D. M., Rush, M. C., & Lance, C. E. (1999). Motivational bases of affective organizational commitment: A partial test of an integrative theoretical model. *Journal of Occupational and Organizational Psychology, 72*(4), 463–483.

English, F. W. (1992). Corporate America's prescription for public education. *International Journal of Educational Reform 1*(2), 134–138.

Epstein, J. (1990). School and family connections: Theory, research, and implications for integrating sociologies of education and family. *Marriage and Family Review, 15,* 99–126.

Ericsson, K. A., Drampe, R. T., & Tesch-Romer, C. (1993). The role of deliberate practices in the acquisition of expert performance. *Psychological Review, 100*(3), 363–406.

Ericsson, K. A., & Smith, J. (1991). *Towards a general theory of expertise.* Cambridge: Cambridge University Press.

Ewell, P. T. (1999, November/December). Imitation as art: Borrowed management techniques in higher education. *Change,* 11–15.

Fagin, C. M. (1997). The leadership role of a dean. In M. J. Austin, F. L. Ahearn, & R. A. English (Eds.), *The professional dean: Meeting the leadership challenges* (Vol. 25). San Francisco: Jossey-Bass.

Fisher, C., & Gitelson, R. (1983). A meta-analysis of the correlates of role conflict and ambiguity. *Journal of Applied Psychology, 68,* 320–333.

Folger, R., & Konovsky, M. A. (1989). Effects of procedural and distributive justice on reactions to pay raise decisions. *Academy of Management Journal, 32,* 115–130.

Forbes, J. B., & Piercy, J. E. (1991). *Corporate mobility and paths to the top: Studies for human resource and management development specialists.* Westport, CT: Quorum Books.

Franklin, J. H. (1993). *The color line: Legacy for the twenty-first century.* Columbia: University of Missouri Press.

French, J., & Caplan, R. (1972). Organizational stress and individual strain. In A. Marrow (Ed.), *The failure of success* (pp. 30–66). New York: Amacom.

Fried, Y., & Tiegs, R. (1995). Supervisors' role conflict and role ambiguity differential relations with performance ratings of subordinates and the moderating effect of screening ability. *Journal of Applied Psychology, 80*(2), 282–291.

Friedman, S. D., Christensen, P., & DeGroot, J. (1998, November/December). Work and life: The end of the zero-sum game. *Harvard Business Review,* 119–129.

Fullan, M. (1991). *The new meaning of educational change.* New York: Teachers College Press.

Gabarro, J. J. (1985, May–June). When a new manager takes charge. *Harvard Business Review,* 110–123.

Gabarro, J. J. (1987). *The dynamics of taking charge*. Boston: Harvard Business School Press.

Gardner, J. W. (1987). *Leadership development*. Washington, DC: Independent Sector.

Gardner, J. W. (1990). *On leadership*. New York: Free Press.

Gattiker, U. E., & Larwood, L. (1990). Prediction of career achievement in the corporate hierarchy. *Human Relation, 43*, 703–726.

Getzels, J. (1952). A psycho-sociological framework or the study of educational administration. *Harvard Educational Review, 22*, 235–246.

Gherardi, S. (1995). *Gender, symbolism, and organizational cultures*. Newbury Park, CA: Sage.

Glazer-Raymo, J. (1999). *Shattering the myths: Women in academe*. Baltimore: Johns Hopkins University Press.

Gmelch, W. H. (1989). *A conceptual understanding of administrative stress*. Paper presented at the AERA Conference, San Diego.

Gmelch, W. H. (2000a). Leadership succession: How new deans take charge and learn the job. *Journal of Leadership Studies, 7*(3), 68–87.

Gmelch, W. H. (2000b). *Rites of passage: Transition to the deanship*. Paper presented at the American Association of Colleges for Teacher Education Conference, Chicago.

Gmelch, W. H., & Burns, J. S. (1994). Sources of stress for academic department chairpersons. *Journal of Educational Administration. 32*(1), 79–94.

Gmelch, W. H., & Chan, W. (1994). *Thriving on stress for success*. Thousand Oaks, CA: Corwin Press.

Gmelch, W. H., Lovrich, N. P., & Wilke, P. K. (1984). Stress in academe: A national perspective. *Review of Higher Education, 20*(4), 477–490.

Gmelch, W. H., & Miskin, V. D. (1993). *Strategic leadership skills for department chairs*. Boston: Anker.

Gmelch, W. H., & Miskin, V. D. (1995). *Chairing an academic department*. Newbury Park, CA: Sage.

Gmelch, W. H., & Parkay, F. W. (1999). *Becoming a department chair: Negotiating the transition from scholar to administrator*. Paper presented at the annual meeting of the American Educational Research Association, Montreal.

Gmelch, W. H., & Seedorf, R. (1989). Academic leadership under siege: The ambiguity and imbalance of department chairs. *Journal for Higher Education Management, 5*, 37–44.

Gmelch, W. H., Wilke, P. K., & Lovrich, N. P. (1986). Dimensions of stress among university faculty: Factor analytic results from a national study. *Research in Higher Education, 24*(3), 266–286.

Gmelch, W. H., Wolverton, M., & Wolverton, M. L. (1999). *The education dean's search for balance*. Paper presented at the American Association of Colleges of Teacher Education Conference, Washington, DC.

Gmelch, W. H., Wolverton, M., Wolverton, M. L., & Hermanson, M. (1996). *National study of academic deans in higher education.* Pullman, WA: Center for Academic Leadership.

Gmelch, W. H., Wolverton, M., Wolverton, M. L., & Sarros, J. C. (1999). The academic dean: An imperiled species searching for balance. *Research in Higher Education, 40*(6), 717– 740.

Gould, R. L. (1978). *Transformations: Growth and change in adult life.* New York: Simon & Schuster.

Grace, H. K. (1982). The dean as scholar: Clinical competence, teaching, research, and publication. Washington, DC: American Association of Colleges of Nursing.

Graves, S. B. (1990). A case of double jeopardy? Black women in higher education. *Initiatives, 53,* 3–8.

Green, M. F., & McDade, S. A. (1994). *Investing in higher education: A handbook of leadership development.* Phoenix, AZ: Oryx Press.

Green, S. G., Anderson, S. E., & Shivers, S. L. (1996). Demographic and organizational influences on leader-member exchange and related work attitudes. *Organizational Behavior and Human Decision Processes, 66*(2), 203–214.

Greenleaf, R. K. (1977) *Servant leadership.* New York: Paulist Press.

Griffiths, D. E. (1966). *The school superintendent.* New York: The Center for Applied Research in Education.

Griffiths, D. E., & McCarty, D. J. (Eds.). (1980). *The dilemma of the deanship.* Danville, IL: Interstate.

Gross, N., Mason, W., & McEachern, A. (1958). *Explorations in role analysis: Studies of the school superintendent role.* New York: Wiley.

Gupta, N., & Beehr, T. A. (1979). Job stress and employee behavior. *Organizational Behavior and Human Performance, 23,* 373–387.

Guskin, A. E. (1994a, July/August). Reducing student costs and enhancing student learning: The university challenge of the 1990s. Part I: Restructuring the administration. *Change,* 23–29.

Guskin, A. E. (1994b, September/October). Reducing student costs and enhancing student learning: The university challenges of the 1990s. Part II: Restructuring the role of faculty. *Change,* 16–25.

Guskin, A. E. (1996, July/August). Facing the future: The change process in restructuring universities. *Change,* 26–37.

Hagedorn, L. S. (1996). Wage equity and female faculty job satisfaction: The role of wage differentials in a job satisfaction causal model. *Research in Higher Education 37*(5), 569– 598.

Hall, M. R. (1993). *The dean's role in fund raising.* Baltimore: Johns Hopkins University Press.

Hart, A. W. (1993). Leader succession and socialization: A synthesis. *Review of Educational Research, 61*(4), 451–474.

Hearst Newspapers. (1999, March 18). Student leaders' parents vital to success. *Spokesman Review*, p. A8.

Hecht, I.W.D., Higgerson, M. L., Gmelch, W. H., and Tucker, A. (1999). *The department chair as cademic leader*. Phoenix, AZ: American Council on Education, Oryx Press.

Heifetz, R. A. (1994). *Leadership without easy answers*. Cambridge, MA: Harvard University Press.

Helgesen, S. (1990). *The female advantage: Women's ways of leadership*. New York: Doubleday/Currency.

Helgesen, S. (1995). *The web of inclusion*. New York: Currency/Doubleday.

Heneman, H. G., III, & Schwab, D. P. (1985). Pay satisfaction: Its multi-dimensional nature and measurement. *International Journal of Psychology, 20*, 129–141.

Henry, M. E. (1996). *Parent-school collaboration: Feminist organizational structures and school leadership*. Albany: SUNY Press.

Hersey, P., & Blanchard, K. H. (1988). *The management of organizational behavior*. Englewood Cliffs, NJ: Prentice Hall.

Hersi, D. T. (1993). Factors contributing to job satisfaction for women in higher education administration. *CUPA Journal, 44*(2), 29–35.

Herzberg, F. (1966). *Work and the nature of man*. Cleveland: World.

Hesselbein, F., Goldsmith, M., & Beckhard, R. (Eds.). (1996). *The leader of the future*. San Francisco: Jossey-Bass.

Hewitt, J. P. (1997). *Self and society: A symbolic interactionist social psychology*. Boston: Allyn & Bacon.

Hill, M. S., & Ragland, J. C. (1995). *Women as educational leaders: Opening windows, pushing ceilings*. Thousand Oaks, CA: Corwin Press.

Holland, J. L. (1966). A psychological classification scheme for vocations and major fields. *Journal of Counseling Psychology, 13*, 278–288.

Hollander, E. P. (1964). *Leaders, groups, and influence*. New York: Oxford University Press.

Holt, R. R. (1982). Occupational stress. In L. Goldberger & S. Birznitz (Eds.), *Handbook of stress* (pp. 419–444). New York: Free Press.

House, J. S. (1981). *Work stress and social support*. Reading, MA: Addison-Wesley.

Hubbard, S., & Robinson, J. (1998). Mentoring: A catalyst for advancement in administration. *Journal of Career Development, 24*(4), 289–299.

Hughs, M. S. (1988). Developing leadership potential for minority women. In M. Sagaria (Ed.), *Empowering women: Leadership development strategies on campus* (pp. 63–76). San Francisco: Jossey-Bass.

Hulin, C. L., Roznowski, M., & Hachiya, D. (1985). Alternative opportunities and withdrawal decisions: Empirical and theoretical discrepancies and an integration. *Psychological Bulletin, 97*, 233–250.

Idson, T. L. (1990). Establishment size, job satisfaction, and the structure of work. *Applied Economics, 22*, 1007–1018.

Ivancevich, J. M., & Matteson, M. (1987). *Organizational behavior and management*. Plano, TX: Business.

Jackson, J. (2000). *Decanal work: Using role theory and the sociology of time to study the executive behavior of college of education deans*. Unpublished doctoral dissertation, Iowa State University, Ames.

Jacobs, T. O. (1970). *Leadership and exchange in formal organizations*. Alexandria, VA: Human Resources Research Organization.

Jacobson, R. L. (1994). Wanted: Business deans. *Chronicle of Higher Education*, 40(37), A17– A18.

Jamieson, K. H. (1995). *Beyond the double bind: Women and leadership*. New York: Oxford University Press.

Judge, T., Boudreau, J., & Bretz, R. (1994). Job and life attitudes of male executives. *Journal of Applied Psychology*, 79(5), 767–782.

Judge, T. A., & Hulin, C. L. (1993). Job satisfaction as a reflection of disposition: A multiple source causal analysis. *Organizational Behavior and Human Decision Processes*, 56, 388–421.

Kacmar, K. M., Carlson, D. S., & Brymer, R. A. (1999). Antecedents and consequences of organizational commitment: A comparison of two scales. *Educational and Psychological Measurement*, 59(6), 976–994.

Kahn, R. (1981). *Work and health*. New York: Wiley.

Kahn, R., & Byosiere, P. (1992). Stress in organizations. In M. Dunnette & L. Hough (Eds.), *Handbook of industrial and organizational psychology* (Vol. 3). Palo Alto, CA: Consulting Psychologists Press.

Kahn, R., Wolfe, D. M., Quinn, R. P., & Snoek, J. D. (1964). *Organizational stress: Studies in role conflict and ambiguity*. New York: Wiley.

Kanter, R. M. (1977). *Men and women of the corporation*. New York: Basic Books.

Karsten, M. F. (1994). *Management and gender: Issues and attitudes*. Westport, CT: Praeger.

Katzenbach, J. R. (1998). *Teams at the top: Unleashing the potential of both teams and individual leaders*. Boston: Harvard Business School Press.

Kellerman, B. (1999). *Reinventing leadership*. Albany: SUNY Press.

Kerr, C., with Gade, M., & Kawaoka, M. (1994a). *Higher education cannot escape history: Issues for the twenty-first century*. Albany: State University of New York.

Kerr, C., with Gade, M., & Kawaoka, M. (1994b). *Troubled time for American higher education: The 1990s and beyond*. Albany: State University of New York.

Kleon, S., & Rinehart, S. (1998). Leadership skill development of teen leaders. *Journal of Extension*, 36(3), 157–164.

Koestenbaum, P. (1991). Leadership: *The inner side of greatness*. San Francisco: Jossey-Bass.

Konrad, A. M., & Pfeffer, J. (1991). Understanding the hiring of women and minorities in educational institutions. *Sociology of Education*, 64, 141–157.

Korschgen, A., Fuller, R., & Gardner, J. (2001). The impact of presidential migration: Raising questions about presidential tenure in higher education. *AAHE Bulletin, 53*(6), 3–6.

Kotter, J. (1990a). *A force for change: How leadership differs from management.* New York: Free Press.

Kotter, J. (1990b, May/June). What leaders really do. *Harvard Business Review,* pp. 103–111.

Kouzes, J. M., & Posner, B.Z. (1987). *The leadership challenge.* San Francisco: Jossey-Bass.

Kouzes, J. M., & Posner, B. Z. (1993). *Credibility: How leaders gain and lose it, why people demand it.* San Francisco: Jossey-Bass.

Kouzes, J. M., & Posner, B. Z. (1995). *The leadership challenge: How to keep getting extraordinary things done in organizations.* San Francisco: Jossey-Bass.

Kuhn, T. S. (1970). *The structure of scientific revolution.* Chicago: University of Chicago Press.

Kulik, C. T., Oldham, G. R., & Hackman, J. R. (1987). Work design as an approach to person-environment fit. *Journal of Vocational Behavior, 31,* 278–296.

Lamoreaux, D. (1990). *New shoes: An educational criticism of a new principal's first quarter.* Paper presented at the annual meeting of the American Educational Research Association, Boston.

Lankard, B. A. (1995). *Family role in career development.* ERIC Digest No. 164. Washington DC: Office of Educational Research and Improvement.

LaRocco, J. M., House, J. S., & French, J.R.P., Jr. (1980). Social support, occupational stress, and health. *Journal of Health and Social Behavior 21,* 202–218.

Latta, G. F. (1996). *The virtual university: Creating an emergent reality.* Washington, DC: ERIC.

Layzell, D., Lovell, C., & Gill, J. (1996, March). Developing faculty as an asset in a period of change and uncertainty. In *Integrating research on faculty: Seeking new ways to communicate about the academic life of faculty.* Washington, DC: U.S. Department of Education, National Center for Education Statistics.

Lazarus, R. S. (1966). *Psychological stress and the coping process.* New York: McGraw-Hill.

Lazarus, R. S. (1979, November). Positive denial: the case for not facing reality. *Psychology Today,* 44–60.

Lazarus, R. S., & DeLongis, A. (1983). Psychological stress and coping in aging. *American Psychologist 3:* 245–254.

Lazarus, R. S., & Launier, R. (1978). Stress-related transactions between person and environment. In L. A. Pervin & M. Lewis (Eds.), *Perspectives in interactional psychology.* New York: Plenum.

Lee, D. E. (1985). Department chairpersons' perceptions of the role in three institutions. *Perception and Motor Skills, 61,* 23–49.

Levine, A., & Cureton, J. S. (1998). Collegiate life: An obituary. *Change, 30*(3), 12–17.

Levine, S., & Scotch, N. A. (1970). *Social stress.* Chicago: Aldine.

Levinson, D. J. (1978). *The season's of a man's life.* New York: Knopf.

Levy, M. J. (1952). *The structure of society.* Princeton, NJ: Princeton University Press.

Lewin, K. (1948). *Selected papers on group dynamics.* New York: Harper, 1935–1946.

Lewis, C. T., Garcia, J. E., & Jobs, S. M. (1990). *Managerial skills in organizations.* Boston: Allyn & Bacon.

Lindberg, R. E. (1995). Seeking the elusive balance. *Association Management,* pp. 86–92.

Louis, M. R. (1980). Surprise and sense making: What newcomers experience in entering unfamiliar organizational settings. *Administrative Science Quarterly, 25,* 226–251.

Lucas, A. F. (1994). *Strengthening department leadership.* San Francisco: Jossey-Bass.

Lucas, A. F. (2000). *Leading academic change: Essential roles for department chairs.* San Francisco: Jossey-Bass.

Maccoby, M. (1981). *The leader: A new face for American management.* New York: Simon & Schuster.

March, J. G., & Simon, H. A. (1958). *Organizations.* New York: Wiley.

Martin, J. L. (1993). *Academic deans: An analysis of effective academic leadership at research universities.* Paper presented at the annual meeting of the American Educational Research Association, Atlanta.

Mathieu, J. E., & Hamel, K. (1989). A causal model of antecedents of organizational commitment among professional and nonprofessionals. *Journal of Vocational Behavior, 34,* 299–317.

Mathieu, J. E., & Zajac, D. (1990). A review and meta-analysis of the antecedents, correlates, and consequences of organizational commitment. *Psychological Bulletin, 108,* 171–194.

Matteson, M. T., & Ivancevich, J. M. (1987). *Controlling work stress: Effective human resource and management strategies.* San Francisco: Jossey-Bass.

Matusak, L. R. (1997). *Finding your voice: Learning to lead . . . anywhere you want to make a difference.* San Francisco: Jossey-Bass.

Mau, W. (1997). Parental influences on the high school students' academic achievement: A comparison of Asian immigrants, Asian American, and white Americans. *Psychology in the Schools, 34*(3), 267–277.

McBride, S. A., Munday, R. G., & Tunnell, J. (1992). Community college faculty satisfaction and propensity to leave. *Community/Junior College Quarterly, 16,* 157–165.

McCarty, D. J., & Reyes, P. (1987). Organizational models of governance: Academic deans' decision-making styles. *Journal of Teacher Education, 38*(5), 2–8.

McCracken, D. M. (2000, November/December). Winning the talent war for women: Sometimes it takes a revolution. *Harvard Business Review*, pp. 159–168.

McGrath, J. E. (1999). The dean. *Journal of Higher Education, 70*(5), 599–605. (Original work published in 1936)

McGrath, J. E. (1976). Stress and behavior in organizations. In D. M. Dunnette, *The handbook of industrial and organizational psychology*. Chicago: Rand McNally.

McLaughlin, G. W., Montgomery, J. R., & Malpass, L. F. (1975). Selected characteristics, roles, goals and satisfactions of department chairmen in state and land-grant institutions. *Research in Higher Education, 3*, 243–259.

Merton, R. (1957). The role-set. *British Journal of Sociology, 8*, 106–120.

Meyer, J. P., & Allen, N. J. (1991). A three-component conceptualization of organizational commitment. *Human Resource Management Review, 1*(1), 61–89.

Meyer, J. P., & Allen, N. J. (1997). *Commitment in the workplace: Theory, research, and application*. Thousand Oaks, CA: Sage.

Mintzberg, H. (1973). *The nature of managerial work*. New York: Harper & Row.

Mintzberg, H. (1983). *Structure in fives: Designing effective organizations*. Englewood Cliffs, NJ: Prentice Hall.

Mintzberg, H. (1998, November/December). Covert leadership: Notes on managing professionals. *Harvard Business Review*, pp. 140–147.

Moore, D. (1992). The case for parent and community involvement. In G.A. Hess (Ed.), *Empowering teachers and parents: School restructuring through the eyes of anthropologists*. Westport, CT: Bergin & Garvey.

Moore, K. M. (1990 Winter). Creating strengths out of our differences: Women and minority administrators. *New Directions for Higher Education, 72*, 89–98.

Moore, K. M., & Amey, M. J. (1988). Some faculty leaders are born women. In M. Sagaria (Ed.), *Empowering women: Leadership development strategies on campus* (pp. 39–50). San Francisco: Jossey-Bass.

Moore, K. M., Salimbene, A. M., Marlier, J. D., & Bragg, S. M. (1983). The structure of presidents' and deans' careers. *Journal of Higher Education, 54*(5), 500–515.

Morris, V. C. (1981). *Deaning: Middle management in academe*. Urbana: University of Illinois Press.

Morrison, A. (1996). *The new leaders: Leadership diversity in America*. San Francisco: Jossey-Bass.

Mortenson, T. G. (1994a, September). Part-time college enrollment: It's mostly a matter of age. *Postsecondary Education Opportunity, 27*, 1–19.

Mortenson, T. G. (1994b, October). Raising tuition . . . to build prisons: Infatuation with incarceration. *Postsecondary Education Opportunity, 28*, 7–13.

Mowday, R. T., Porter, L. W., & Steers, R. M. (1982). *Employee-organization linkages: The psychology of commitment, absenteeism, and turnover.* New York: Academic Press.

Mowday, R. T., Steers, R. M., & Porter, L. W. (1979). The measurement of organizational commitment. *Journal of Vocational Behavior, 14,* 224–247.

Nash, A. M. (1994). *An exploration of job satisfaction, life satisfaction, and organizational commitment.* Unpublished master's thesis, Washington State University, Pullman, WA.

Neumann, Y., & Boris, S. B. (1978). Paradigm development and leadership style of university department chairpersons. *Research in Higher Education, 9,* 291–302.

Newcomb, T. M. (1950). *Social psychology.* New York: Dryden.

Nicholson, N., & West, M. (1989). Transitions, work histories, and careers. In M. B. Arthur, D. T. Hall, & B. S. Laurence (Eds.), *Handbook of career theory* (pp. 181–201). New York: Cambridge University Press.

Oakes, J. L. (1999). Women as capable leaders in higher education administration: A historical journey with implications for professional mentoring. *A Leadership Journal: Women in Leadership—Sharing the Vision, 3*(2), 57–62.

Okagaki, L., & Sternberg, R. J. (1993). Parental beliefs and children's school performance. *Child Development 64,* 35–56.

O'Reilly, B. (August 8, 1994). What's killing the business school dean of America? *Fortune,* 64–68.

Ortiz, F. I. (1982). *Career patterns in education.* New York: Praeger.

O'Toole, J. (1995). *Leading change.* San Francisco: Jossey-Bass.

Parkay, F. W., & Hall, G. E. (1992). *Becoming a principal: The challenges of beginning leadership.* Boston, MA: Allyn & Bacon.

Peters, T., & Waterman, R. J. (1982). *In search of excellence: Lessons from America's best-run companies.* New York: Warner Books.

Pettigrew, T. F., & Martin, J. (1987). Shaping the organizational context for black American inclusion. *Journal of Social Issues, 43*(1), 41–78.

Pew Policy Perspectives. (1996). *Double agent.* Philadelphia: Institute for Research on Higher Education.

Pfeffer, J., & Langton, N. (1993). The effect of wage dispersion on satisfaction, productivity, and working collaboratively: Evidence from college and university faculty. *Administrative Science Quarterly, 38,* 382–407.

Phillipps, D., & Thomas, A. R. (1983). Profile of a principal under stress. *Primary Education, 14*(6), 6–8, 31.

Porter, L. W., & Steers, R. M. (1973). Organizational, work, and personal factors in employee turnover and absenteeism. *Psychological Bulletin, 80*(2), 151–176.

Porter, L. W., Steers, R. M., Mowday, R. T., & Boulian, P. (1974). Organizational commitment, job satisfaction, and turnover among psychiatric technicians. *Journal of Applied Psychology, 59*(5), 603–609.

Posig, M. (1999). Role investment and gender: A work-family issue. *A Leadership Journal: Women in Leadership–Sharing the Vision 3*(2), 43–55.

Pulling, J. (1989). We can learn from business—And teach a thing or two. *Executive Education 11*(4), 32–33.

Quinn, R. E., Faerman, S. R., Thompson, M. P., & McGrath, M. R. (1990). *Becoming a master manager: A competency framework.* New York: Wiley.

Ready, D. (1994). *Champions of change.* Lexington, MA: International Consortium for Executive Development Research.

Regan, H. B., & Brooks, G. H. (1995). *Out of women's experience: Creating relational leadership.* Thousand Oaks, CA: Corwin Press.

Reichers, A. E. (1986). Conflict and organizational commitments. *Journal of Applied Psychology, 71*(3), 508–514.

Rizzo, J. R., House, R. J., & Lirtzman, S. I. (1970). Role conflict and ambiguity in complex organizations. *Administrative Science Quarterly, 15*, 150–163.

Ronen, S. (1986). Equity perception in multiple comparisons: A field study. *Personnel Psychology, 39*, 333–346.

Rosenbach, W. E., & Sashkin, M. (1995). *Leadership inventory.* Gettysburg, PA: Gettysburg College Eisenhower Leadership Program.

Rost, J. C. (1993). *Leadership for the twenty-first century.* Westport, CT: Praeger.

Ryan, D. (1980). Deans as individuals in organizations. In D. Griffith & D. McCarty (Eds.), *The dilemma of the deanship.* Danville, IL: Interstate.

Sanders, K. W., & Mellow, G. O. (1990). Permanent diversity: The deferred vision of higher education. *Initiatives, 53*, 9–13.

Sargent, S. (1951). Concepts of role and ego in contemporary psychology. In J. Rohru & M. Sherif (Eds.), *Social Psychology at the Crossroads.* New York: Harper & Brothers.

Sarros, J. C., & Gmelch, W. H. (1996). *The role of the department head in Australian universities.* Melbourne, Australia: Monash University.

Sarros, J. C., Gmelch, W. H., & Tanewski, G. A. (1996). *Role stress and satisfaction of academic department heads.* Frankston, Victoria, Australia: Monash University.

Schaubroeck, J., Cotton, J., & Jennings, K. (1989). Antecedents and consequences of role stress: A covariance structure analysis. *Journal of Organizational Behavior, 10*, 35–58.

Schein, E. (1992). *Organizational culture and leadership* (2nd ed.). San Francisco: Jossey-Bass.

Scholl, R. W., Cooper, E. A., & McKenna, J. F. (1987). Referent selection in determining equity perceptions: Differential effects on behavioral and attitudinal outcomes. *Personnel Psychology, 40*, 113–124.

Schön, D. A. (1983). *The reflective practitioner: How professionals think in action.* New York: Basic Books.

Schonwetter, D. J., Bond, S. L., & Perry, R. P. (1993). *Women academic and career administrators role perceptions and occupational satisfaction: Implications for appointment and professional development.* Paper presented AERA, Atlanta.

Schwab, R. L., Jackson, S. E., & Schuler, R. S. (1986). Educator burnout: Sources and consequences. *Educational Research Quarterly, 10*(3), 14–30.

Scott, D. K., & Awbrey, S. M. (1993). Transforming scholarship. *Change, 25*(4), 38–43.

Seedorf, R. (1990). *Transition to leadership: The university department chair.* Unpublished doctoral dissertation, Washington State University, Pullman, WA.

Selye, H. (1974). *Stress without distress.* New York: Lippincott.

Selye, H. (1976). *The stress of life* (2nd ed.). New York: McGraw-Hill.

Selznick, P. (1957). *Leadership in administration: A sociological interpretation.* Evanston, IL: Row, Peterson.

Sergiovanni, T. J. (1990). *Value-added leadership.* San Diego: Harcourt Brace Jovanovich.

Sessa, V. I., & Taylor, J. J. (2000). *Executive selection: Strategies for success.* San Francisco: Jossey-Bass.

Shakeshaft, C. (1985). Strategies for overcoming barriers to women in educational administration. In S. S. Klien (Ed.), *Handbook for achieving sex equality through education.* Baltimore: Johns Hopkins University Press.

Sheehy, G. (1976). *Passages: Predictable crises of adult life.* New York: Dutton.

Sheehy, G. (1995). *New passages: Mapping your life across time.* New York: Random House.

Sherman, S. (1996, March 18). Secrets of H-P's 'muddled' team. *Fortune,* 116–120.

Sherman, S. (1995, December 11). Wanted: Company change agents. *Fortune,* 197–198.

Shore, L. M., & Tetrick, L. E. (1991). A construct validity study of the Survey of Perceived Organizational Support. *Journal of Applied Psychology, 76,* 637–643.

Smith, P. C., Kendall, L. M., & Hulin, C. L. (1969). *The measurement of satisfaction in work and retirement.* Chicago: Rand McNally.

Smith, T. E. (1991). Agreement of adolescent educational expectations with perceived maternal and paternal educational goals. *Youth and Society 23,* 155–174.

Smulyan, L. (2000). *Balancing acts: Women principals at work.* Albany: SUNY Press.

Stanton, T. H. (1990). *Maintaining the federal government's commitment to education: The case for preserving the deduction for state and local income and property taxes.* Washington, DC: AASA, AASCU, AAUP, ACE,

AFT, ALA, ACCT, ACU, CSY, CCSSO, CGCS, NAESP, NASULGO, NEA, NPTA, NSBA. (Eric Document No. 328 948)

Steele, C. M., & Aronson, J. (1995). Stereotype threat and the intellectual test performance of African Americans. *Journal of Personality and Social Psychology, 69*(5), 613–629.

Stein, R. H., & Trachtenberg, S. J. (Eds.). (1993). *The art of hiring in America's colleges & universities.* Buffalo, NY: Prometheus Books.

Summers, T. P., & Hendrix, W. H. (1991). Modeling the role of pay equity perceptions: A field study. *Journal of Occupational Psychology, 64,* 145–157.

Sutherland, V. J., & Cooper, C. J. (1988). Sources of work stress. In J. J. Hurrell, Jr., L. R. Murphy, & S. L. Souter (Eds.), *Occupational stress: Issues and development in research* (pp. 3–40). New York: Taylor & Francis.

Tack, M. W., & Patitu, C. L. (1992). *Faculty job satisfaction: Women and minorities in peril. ASHE-ERIC higher education report no. 4.* Washington, DC: George Washington University School of Education and Human Development.

Tannen, D. (1990). *You just don't understand: Women and men in conversation.* New York: Ballantine Books.

Tannen, D. (1994). *Talking from 9 to 5: Women and men in the workplace: Language, sex and power.* New York: Avon Books.

Tedrow, B., & Rhoads, R. A. (1999). A qualitative study of women's experiences in community college leadership positions. *Community College Review 27*(3), 1–18.

Tett, R. P., & Meyer, J. P. (1993). Job satisfaction, organizational commitment, turnover intention, and turnover: A path analysis based on meta-analytic findings. *Personnel Psychology, 46,* 259–293.

Tharenou, P., Latimer, S., & Conway, D. (1984). How do you make it to the top? An examination of influences on women's and men's managerial advancement. *Academy of Management Journal, 37*(4), 899–931.

Thomas, D. A. (1990). The impact of race on managers' experiences of developmental relationships. *Journal of Organizational Behavior, 2*(4), 479–492.

Thomas, D. A. (1993). Racial dynamics in cross-race developmental relationships. *Administrative Science Quarterly, 38*(2), 169–194.

Thomas, D. A., & Gabarro, J. J. (1999). *Breaking through: The making of minority executives in corporate America.* Boston: Harvard Business School Press.

Tinley, J. (1994). *Genderflex: Men and women speaking each other's language at work.* New York: AMACOM.

Tucker, A., & Bryan, R. A. (1988). *The academic dean: Dove, dragon and diplomat.* New York: American Council on Education and Macmillan.

Tucker, R. C. (1981). *Politics as leadership.* Columbia: University of Missouri Press.

Turner, C.S.V., Myers, S. L., & Creswell, J. W. (1997). *Bittersweet success: Faculty of color in academe*. University of Nebraska, unpublished manuscript.

Twale, D., & Jelenik, S. (1996). Proteges and mentors: Mentoring experiences of women student affairs professionals. *NASPA Journal, 33*, 203–217.

Twombly, S. B. (1986). *Theoretical approaches to the study of career mobility*. Paper presented at the meeting of the American Educational Research Association, San Francisco.

Twombly, S. B. (1992). The process of choosing a dean. *Journal of Higher Education, 63*(6), 653–683.

U.S. Department of Labor. (1991). *Report on the glass ceiling initiative*. Washington DC: U.S. Government Printing Office.

Vandenberg, R. J., & Lance, C. E. (1992). Examining the causal order of job satisfaction and organizational commitment. *Journal of Management, 18*(1), 153–167.

Van der Werf, M. (1999, September 3). A vice-president from the business world brings a new bottom line to Penn. *Chronicle of Higher Education*, pp. A52–A75.

van Gennep, A. (1960). *Rites of passage*. Trans. M. B. Vizedom & G. L. Chaffee. Chicago: University of Chicago Press.

Vroom, V. H. (1964). *Work and motivation*. New York: Wiley.

Wah, L. (1998). Why there are so few women CEOs. *Management Review, 87*(7), 8–9.

Warner, R., & DeFleur, L. B. (1993). Career paths of women in higher education administration. In P. R. Mitchell (Ed.), *Cracking the wall: Women in higher education administration* (pp. 1–18). Washington, DC: College and University Personnel Association.

Weindling, D., & Early, P. (1987). *Secondary leadership: The first years*. Philadelphia: NFER-Nelson.

Welsch, H. P., & LaVan, H. (1981). Inter-relationships between organizational commitment and job characteristics, job satisfaction, professional behavior, and organizational climate. *Human Relations, 34*, 1079–1089.

West, C. (1993). *Race matters*. New York: Vintage Books.

Westley, F. (1992). Vision worlds: Strategic visions as social interaction. *Advances in Strategic Management, 8*, 271–305.

Whan, L. D. (1988). *Stress in primary school principals*. Unpublished doctoral dissertation, University of New England, Armidale, Australia.

Wheatley, M. J. (1992). *Leadership and the new science: Learning about organization from an orderly universe*. San Francisco: Berrett-Koehler.

Williams, J. E., & Best, D. L. (1990). *Managing sex stereotypes: A multicultural study*. Newbury Park, CA: Sage.

Winters, W. (1993). *African American mothers and urban schools: The power of participation*. New York: Lexington Books.

Wisniewski, R. (1998). The new Sisyphus: The dean as change agent. In D. Thiessen & K. R. Howey (Eds.), *Agents, provocateurs: Reform-minded leaders for schools of education.* Washington, DC: American Association of Colleges for Teacher Education.

Wolverton, M. (1998). Champions of change, change agents, and collaborators in change: Leadership keys to successful systemic change. *Journal of Higher Education Policy & Management, 20*(1), 19–30.

Wolverton, M., Gmelch, W. H., Montez, J., & Nies, C. T. (2001). *The changing nature of the academic deanship.* San Francisco: Jossey-Bass.

Wolverton, M., Gmelch, W. H., & Sorenson, D. (1998). The department as double agent: The call for departmental change and renewal. *Innovative Higher Education, 22*(3), 203–215.

Wolverton, M., Gmelch, W. H., & Wolverton, M. L. (2000). Finding a better person-environment fit in the academic deanship. *Innovative Higher Education, 24*(3), 203–226.

Wolverton, M., Gmelch, W. H., Wolverton, M. L., & Sarros, J. C. (1999). Stress in academic leadership: U.S. and Australian department chairs/heads. *The Review of Higher Education, 22*(2), 165–185.

Wolverton, M., & Gonzales, M. J. (2000). *Career paths of academic deans.* Paper presented at the annual meeting of the American Educational Research Association, New Orleans.

Wolverton, M., Montez, J., & Gmelch, W. H. (2000). *The roles and challenges of deans.* Paper presented at the annual meeting of the Association for the Study of Higher Education, Sacramento.

Wolverton, M., & Poch, S. (2000). The nexus between academic deans and corporate CEOs: An opportunity in the making. *Journal of Leadership Studies, 7*(3), 122–132.

Wolverton, M., Wolverton, M. L., & Gmelch, W. H. (1999). The impact of role conflict and ambiguity on academic deans. *Journal of Higher Education, 70*(1), 80–106.

Woods, P. (1992). Symbolic interactionism: Theory and method. In M. LeCompte, W. Millroy & J. Preissle (Eds.). *The handbook of qualitative research in education* (pp. 337–404). New York: Academic Press.

Yukl, G. (1998). *Leadership in organizations* (4th ed.). Upper Saddle River, NJ: Prentice Hall.

Zaleznik, A. (1989). *The managerial mystique: Restoring leadership in business.* New York: Harper & Row.

INDEX

About the Authors

MIMI WOLVERTON is Associate Professor at the University of Nevada, Las Vegas and co-directs the UCEA Center for Academic Leadership. Wolverton serves on the review board of *Innovative Higher Education* and is editor of the *ASHE Newsletter*.

WALTER H. GMELCH is Dean of the College of Education at Iowa State University, Ames.